PANOS

– LISTENING –
FOR A CHANGE

ORAL TESTIMONY AND DEVELOPMENT

HUGO SLIM and PAUL THOMPSON

Contributing Editors: OLIVIA BENNETT and NIGEL CROSS

Published by Panos Publications Ltd
9 White Lion Street
London N1 9PD, UK

British Library Cataloguing in Publication Data.
Slim, Hugo
Listening for a Change: Oral Testimony and Development
I. Title II. Thompson, Paul
III. Bennett, Olivia IV. Cross, Nigel
907.2
ISBN 1-870670-31-0

Funding for *Listening for a Change* was provided mainly by HelpAge International, Christian Aid, Save the Children Fund (UK), Norwegian Church Aid, The Rowan Trust and the Thomas Sivewright Catto Charitable Settlement, with additional contributions from Trocaire, Scottish Catholic International Aid Fund (SCIAF) and the World Wide Fund for Nature (UK).

Any judgements expressed in this document should not be taken to represent the views of any funding agency. Signed articles do not necessarily relect the views of Panos or any of its funding agencies.

Panos London is an independent information organisation working internationally for development that is socially, environmentally and economically sustainable. Panos also has offices in Paris and Washington DC.

For more information about Panos contact:
Juliet Heller, Panos London

Managing Editor: Olivia Bennett
Production: Sally O'Leary
Cover design: The Graphic Partnership
Printed in Great Britain by Bell and Bain, Glasgow

CONTENTS

ACKNOWLEDGEMENTS

Many people have shared their ideas and experience with us during the writing of this book, and our special thanks go to Hugh Brody, Ben Burt, Robert Chambers, Dwight Conquergood, Ana Dourado, Mark Gorman, Anil Gupta, Kelly Haggart, Craig Johnson, Martha Johnson, Deborah Kasente, Anne LaFond, Alex Mavro, Sara Pait, Kat Payne, Suzanne Quinney, Ian Scoones, Ivan Scott, Megan Vaughan, Alex de Waal, Kitty Warnock, Helen Watson and Ken Wilson. In addition, I would like to thank several of my colleagues at Save the Children Fund, in particular Mike Edwards, Neil MacDonald and Andrew Timpson, for their support and encouragement during the past year.

I am especially grateful to my co-author Paul Thompson who first suggested that we hold a conference on the subject of Oral History and Development. This took place in November 1991 at the National Life Story Collection (NLSC) and led to the decision to write this book. Paul's ideas and enthusiasm have been a great encouragement, while his expertise in the field of oral history has been indispensible. My thanks are also due to Save the Children Fund and Oxfam, who funded the original conference, all those at NLSC who helped to organise it, Jo Bexley at Panos who secured funding for the book, and the donors who agreed to support its publication and dissemination.

I would also like to acknowledge the important role of our two Contributing Editors. Olivia Bennett edited the book, and helped research and write many of the project examples. Nigel Cross gave valuable advice on the text and his contributions include a major case study.

Most of all I would like to thank my friend and former colleague John Mitchell, who has always understood the immense value of listening in development, and who first introduced me to this way of working. If I had not worked alongside him and benefited from his knowledge and experience, this book would not have happened. In this context, I would also like to thank Molla Asnake, Belay Bekele, Tesfabruck Gabremichael and Tekola Kidane for the many times they have listened and interpreted for me in Ethiopia.

Finally, I would like to thank my wife, Rebecca Abrams, whose own experience and expertise in oral history has taught me much, and whose support at every stage of this project has been invaluable.

Hugo Slim
Oxford, October 1993

The Authors

Hugo Slim is the Senior Research Officer for the Save the Children Fund (UK). During his 10-year career in development he has worked for Save the Children, the United Nations, Oxfam and Comic Relief in Ethiopia, Sudan, Morocco, Bangladesh and the Occupied Territories. He is also the co-founder of Rural Evaluations, a consultancy group specialising in the collection of oral testimony of people living in relief and development project areas. He has published widely in development journals and is the co-author of *Registration in Emergencies, Oxfam's Practical Health Guide No 6*.

Paul Thompson is Research Professor at the University of Essex and director of the National Life Story Collection. A pioneer of the oral history movement in Europe, he has taught and researched with life story interviews for 20 years. He has also lectured in China, Russia, Mexico and Brazil. His books include *The Edwardians* and *The Myths We Live By*, as well as *The Voice of the Past*. He is founder-editor of *Oral History* and more recently of *The International Year Book of Oral History and Life Stories*.

CHAPTER ONE

WORDS FROM THE HEART
The power of oral testimony

Words from the heart are more alive than your scribblings. When we speak, our words burn [1].

There has always been a special power in direct speech. The raw recounting of experience has an authenticity and persuasiveness which it is hard to match, and most of us would rather hear someone speak directly than read about them through another's words. Even on the printed page, passages of speech tend to attract our attention: first-person testimony is simply more engaging than impersonal commentary or interpretation.

The spoken word cuts across barriers of wealth, class and race. It is as much the prerogative of ordinary people as of those in positions of power and authority. It requires neither formal education, nor the ability to read and write, nor fluency in any national or official language. Most importantly, it gives voice to the experience of those people whose views are often overlooked or discounted. The significance of this cannot be overestimated. To ignore these voices is to ignore a formidable body of evidence and information.

This book explores ways of listening to the voice and experience of ordinary people. In so doing, it seeks to outline a variety of methods through which those involved in development—from policy makers to project workers—can gain a better understanding of the concerns and priorities, culture and experiences of the people with whom they wish to work. Above all, oral testimony can give those communities more power to set their own agenda for development.

Since much of the book concentrates on the issues which arise from the collection, interpretation and preservation of oral testimony, it is vital to consider how project workers can transmit what they hear and apply what they learn. Without a thorough understanding of the issues involved in this process, listening to people and recording their words can too easily become a purely archival or voyeuristic pursuit, or an exercise in knowledge extraction.

Acting on listening

The role of listener comes with certain obligations. A reciprocal exchange is required in which what is heard is both given back and carried forward. People's testimony must be treated with respect. The origins and ownership of the spoken word should always be honoured, either by recognising authorship or by guaranteeing anonymity.

By applying what is heard in partnership with those who voice it, collecting and communicating oral testimony can become a cooperative exercise in social action. The implications are exciting and far-reaching. It can lead to a critique of development policies, or to improved strategies for responding to famine and refugee crises. It can give rise to a more relevant schools or training curriculum, the evaluation and adaptation of traditional agricultural practices or the mounting of a land rights campaign. It can encourage a more effective response to the particular circumstances of women or improved health care for children or the elderly. Whatever the outcome, it is important that the process of listening does eventually result in acknowledgement and action, and that those who have given up their time to talk, know that their words have been taken seriously. This notion of "applied" oral testimony is what gives the listening process a particular relevance to development and differentiates it from a purely academic study.

Making development accountable

At the heart of this principle of applied oral testimony is a challenge to the development establishment. The inclusion of direct testimony in the development debate can help to make it less of a monologue and more of a dialogue, as people's testimony begins to require answers and as their voices force the development establishment to be more accountable for their actions. In short, it is not enough for the development "expert" to summarise and interpret the views of others—the "others" must be allowed to speak for themselves.

"Accountability" and "transparency" may well be the buzz words of development into the next decade. Bringing the voice and experience of poor people to bear on development issues will, however, be the acid test for whether these words achieve anything more than "buzz" status. A wide variety of development agencies from the World Bank to small non-government organisations (NGOs) are making increasing efforts to canvass the views and opinions of people in areas where they intervene. Such feedback undoubtedly highlights the immense difficulties and complexities inherent in creating sustainable patterns of development. But if these voices are ignored, then much development will continue by default to support or create further inequalities.

The concept of "listening to the people" is by no means new to the development establishment. Participation and consultation have been at the heart of most of what has been considered progressive and effective in the field to date. Similarly, the attempt to be heard is not a new one on the part of the so-called beneficiaries of aid. Over the past three decades of development, they have tried in many ways to raise their voice above the clamour of debate that has raged around them. All too often, however, planners and policy makers hear only what they want to, and adopt methods of listening which ignore the more challenging or awkward views and testimonies. And even if people's attempts to talk and to listen are successful at field level, donors, governments and policy makers still have to be convinced. Without the political will to take account of the results of such an exchange, people will be poorly rewarded for giving others the benefit of their time and thoughts.

A voice in the development debate

Speaking out is an act of power, and the act of listening demands respect for the speaker. But listening is also an art, based on certain fundamental principles which are also at the heart of any notion of just and cooperative development. Interviewing is not just a practical mechanism for gathering information. It needs the human skills of patience, humility,

Eritrean widow and refugee Hawa Filli (right) shows the interviewer a photograph of her husband as she recounts her life story.

willingness to learn from others and to respect views and values which you may not share. As a listener, your sources are not dead documents or statistics, but living people and you have to be able to work together.

Hidden voices

One of the reasons why poor communities are so seldom heard is because of the documentary bias—the bias of the written word—which exists at all the key stages of development planning, implementation and evaluation. People are not consulted enough because the main debates take place in documents which they do not write, or in meetings which they do not attend.

Bringing together what people say and think in the form of oral testimony, and then communicating those testimonies, is one way of correcting a bias which runs through the whole development debate and dictates the majority of development initiatives. It is a way of giving volume and power to the voices of people who are outside the development establishment and of ensuring that they are heard.

If being poor means having less of a voice, then being the poorest of the poor means being the most silent of all. Even

within the ranks of the disadvantaged, there are individuals
and groups who—if they are remembered at all—tend to be
"spoken for" and often misrepresented. The collective voice of
any community tends towards generalisations, simplifications
or half-truths and is dominated by the loudest voices. Like the
official document, the community view will tend to concentrate
on the concerns of the wealthy, the political elite, and social and
religious leaders.

Listening to individual testimonies acts as a counterpoint to
generalisations and provides important touchstones against
which to review the collective version. It gives development
workers access to the views and experience of more
marginalised groups, such as the elderly, women, ethnic
minorities, the disabled and children. Bringing in these hidden
voices allows a much more subtle appreciation of the divisions
and alliances within societies.

Sometimes the hidden voices are the most important of all.
In many societies, it has been common for men to take the
dominant role in public life, but for women to be the anchors of
the household and farm economy. Yet there is an equally
widespread prejudice which tends to reduce what women
speak about to the realm of "gossip", while the same bias
elevates men's talk to the status of serious and constructive
discussion. Indeed, there are important differences in patterns
of talking and listening which affect not only the way in which
men and women talk, but also the times and places in which it
is socially acceptable for them to speak. Men may speak out in
public places, in front of people and in the centre of the town or
village. Women tend to talk together "backstage"—in private
places, in the home or at communal places of work. For men,
talking is often a legitimate and valued activity in itself—a
mark of stature and a social responsibility. For women, talking
is rarely something they can make time to do for its own sake,
but is more often an activity to be carried out alongside
others—while working, cooking, or looking after children.

Thus in many communities, men's social responsibility as the
official communicators permits them to step forward and
"speak for the team", as American socio-linguist Deborah
Tannen has pointed out [2]. This often involves them in
speaking for women about things that they, as men, may know
very little about, such as childrearing, health care, women's

Bolivian women talking while they work. Women's workloads leave little room for meetings and public discussion, whereas male cultures often set aside time and space for communal debate.

roles in agriculture and marketing, fuel and water collection. Men may also speak for women when it is religiously or culturally unacceptable for women to talk to men or strangers.

This gender imbalance between public and private talk means that in most societies men's voices are heard over and above women's, and it makes the role of oral testimony collection even more important as a way of redressing that balance. The relative silence of women in many societies means that listening to them should be a priority. Special attention should be paid to women's oral artistry, which manifests itself most powerfully in working songs, stories and proverbs. Such artistry is particularly resonant of the reality of women's lives, a reality which can never truly be depicted, and is more likely to be distorted, when described by men. In this context—and in all attempts to listen to the hidden voices of society—the words of the American feminist Dale Spender are relevant: "Reality is constructed and sustained primarily by those who talk...those who control the talk are also those who are able to control reality [3]."

At community level, therefore, the testimony of individual voices reveals the experience of hidden groups, and counters the bias of those who speak for or ignore them. It has the capacity to break down generalisations and misinformation about communities, their economies, needs, power structures, social organisation and goals. While this may complicate the design of relief and development projects, it may ultimately make them more equitable and effective.

Hidden spheres

In the same way that oral testimony can give voice to hidden groups, it also provides the opportunity to describe hidden spheres of experience, particularly aspects of private and cultural life which might be missed out in a routine development analysis. Economic factors do not exist in a vacuum. Social relationships reflect and influence economic and political ones, and an improved understanding of the former can shed light on the latter. The various forms of oral testimony give people the chance to voice their experience of family and work relationships, of friendship, love, sexuality, childbirth, parenting and leisure, culture and religion. These aspects of life, which are central to anyone's understanding of his or her world, are often overlooked in project feasibility studies, which tend to take a mechanistic view of communities, their needs and possible solutions. Yet people are more likely to take part in something they value and believe in, and are more willing to invest their time and resources in what is feasible within their current social obligations.

Hidden connections

Individuals' own accounts of their life and experience usually paint a much fuller picture than most development planners and project workers look for. Above all, personal testimonies connect the various spheres of life, such as family and work, or health and income, which professionals tend to separate. Relief and development planning is often affected by a kind of inter-sectoral blindness, the myopia of the specialist. The various technical disciplines or professions of development workers mean that they often tackle community development in sectors: health, agriculture, economics, nutrition, law, psychology and so on. People's first-hand accounts of their life and experience tend to flow to and fro between sectors, and to stress the connections rather than the differences. All aspects of a life are intertwined, but it often takes direct communication, rather than a completed survey form, to remind specialists of this fact.

Such testimony obliges development workers to think across sectors and take an inter-disciplinary approach. As people's experiences of famine testify, food aid is not the clear-cut solution to starvation that it seems. Survival is about much more than material relief (see p30). As women's voices have made clear, the need for supplies of clean water is not just about health, it is about time and labour, distance and power. Personal testimonies about HIV infection and AIDS reveal that the issue is not just medical, and the consequences are not confined to illness, death and grief, but include far wider social and economic costs.

Cooperation, confidence and consciousness

The process of talking and listening is potentially an extremely cooperative and participatory one. If it is going well, people are involved, in the fullest sense, in the narration of their experience and the analysis of their situation. Moreover, the collection, interpretation and presentation of oral testimony can become a genuinely communal venture. In addition to the primary role of narrators, people may also become involved as interviewers, or as interpretors of information, or in the presentation and transmission of their own or others' words through publications, radio, theatre or exhibitions. The collection of oral testimony is a process that can involve a whole community.

Speaking up is a sign of confidence; being listened to increases that confidence. In many projects where people have come together to voice their ideas and experience, an increased sense of community and of social consciousness has emerged. Voicing something begins to make it concrete and therefore more possible. It also starts a process of sharing, and this pooling of experience can in turn generate or strengthen a sense of social cohesion.

The process can be not only therapeutic, but also assertive. People who begin to voice their personal or group experience, can begin to understand it and to act on it. This sense of the spoken word marking the beginning of things is fundamental to many cultures where naming things is often a way of creating them in mythical and religious thought. Equally, on a purely individual and psychological level, speaking about a certain situation is often the first step towards addressing it.

For a group of Guatemalan refugee women in Mexico, narrating their life stories to one another and speaking out about the problems of their isolation was the beginning of a broader mental health programme which eventually supported a wide network of refugee families. In Egypt, a group of migrant women coming to terms with their new life in Cairo's City of the Dead found their regular storytelling sessions, based on their personal histories, played a crucial part in sustaining practical bonds of friendship and support between them and their families [4]. The case study of urban Brazilian communities in Chapter Five illustrates how such a process can mobilise a whole community in a struggle for rights and recognition.

Equal idioms

A central part of any attempt at listening is a commitment to accept the idiom of the people who are talking. This automatically contributes to a more equal relationship. Too often the poor and powerless are further disadvantaged by having to conform to the language and communication methods of those who hold power. Oral testimony reverses this trend. Ideally, it should take place in the speaker's mother tongue and interviewers should respect traditional ways of communicating, instead of imposing "vertical" systems, such as questionnaires and surveys, or insisting on use of the official language. In this way the collection of oral testimony shifts the burden of translation and understanding back to the listener, and begins to balance the scales in the communication process. It gives people the opportunity to express themselves in their own terms, employing their language, relating their history, their stories, traditions, songs, theatre and all that goes to make up the repertoire with which individuals communicate among themselves and with others.

Listening to people's oral testimony involves accepting this kind of "horizontal" communication, and then finding ways of preserving, translating and communicating it onwards to a wider and different audience. The latter process has its risks and pitfalls, but it is at least more equitable than any top-down or non-consultative approach.

Moreover, the process of listening reverses the roles of expert and pupil which have become all too typical of relations between development worker and so-called beneficiary. In collecting oral testimony, the interviewer sits at the feet of people who are obviously the experts on their own life and experience. This role reversal, and the process of listening, can generate greater mutual respect and a more equal and collaborative relationship. SOS Sahel, a development organisation which ran the three-year Sahel Oral History Project (see p126), found that:

> Not the least of the benefits of employing oral history methods in a development context is the impact on project workers, nearly all of whom have acquired valuable new insights....[and have identified the value] of taking the time to learn, through interviews, as much as possible from individual life stories and reflections [5].

Development is not an exact science: to date it has been riddled with misunderstandings, failed experiments and discarded theories. But it is increasingly recognised that one of the most damaging aspects of the aid industry has been the tendency of donors to impose their own theories of what constitutes development on the recipients. This book aims to identify some useful ways in which the voices of ordinary people may "burn" more brightly, so that it is their priorities and concerns which inform the development debate.

CHAPTER TWO

VARIETIES OF ORAL EVIDENCE

There are many forms through which people may express their experiences and transmit interpretations of life: songs and legends, stories and plays; traditional accounts of community or family history passed down from generation to generation; simple personal life stories, recollections and memories. Oral testimonies can be collected individually or in groups. They can focus entirely on the past; or they can provide evidence about more recent events and articulate future plans and aspirations.

Broadly speaking, the different forms can be divided into three groups: oral history, oral tradition (which includes oral artistry) and life stories. For our purposes, these overlapping and closely related categories are often subsumed under the general term "oral testimony", but it is worth understanding some of the different purposes, emphases and techniques in each form of oral evidence.

Oral history

The simplest definition of oral history would be "the living memory of the past". Everyone has a story to tell of his or her own life, which offers invaluable raw material for the history of this century. These stories provide a direct account of times of unprecedented change through the men and women who experienced them. If they remain untapped, such living memories are lost for ever. Since the 1940s, professional historians in the North have been recording them as archives for the future and using them as evidence to complement or counterbalance more traditional or official sources.

While in the North oral history is in this sense one of the newest forms of historical work, it is also the oldest: in both the North and the South, its roots go back as far as can be traced.

The first great "histories" of the ancient world in Europe—by Homer, Herodotus, Tacitus—drew on both oral tradition (stories of the past handed down from generation to generation) and direct personal witness. For before the spread of writing, all social knowledge, including history, had to be handed on from memory by word of mouth.

In the North, the role of oral history in both popular culture and professional practice shrank as literacy spread. It probably reached its lowest point earlier this century, when written or printed communication was paramount. In Britain in the Victorian age, pioneers such as Henry Mayhew in his *London Labour and the London Poor* (1861-62) had shown the extraordinary power of directly quoting the voices of poor women and men in conveying the message of a social inquiry, but such instances remained very rare.

The revival of oral history in the North is a result of two fundamental social changes since the 1940s. The first is in the technology of communication. A hundred years ago, the news and public opinion were conveyed by printed newspaper, and personal thought by letter: even a prime minister might write two dozen letters by hand in a day. But for documenting the present, written documents cannot be enough. In the North today, television, radio, and spoken and visual communication have become more powerful than the printed word. People telephone rather than write letters—and a telephone call leaves no record for the archive. Few people keep regular diaries, beyond noting appointments. Most people watch television for news and entertainment rather than read newspapers and books. And although the success of the fax machine may see some return to writing rather than phoning, the whole balance in communication has shifted back towards the oral and visual. Yet this does not mean that experiences and memories need be lost to the historian or social investigator. On the contrary, these new technologies have brought the tape recorder and video camera, allowing the immense variety of individual experience to be captured with a unique spontaneity and vividness.

The second fundamental change in the North was the arrival of a democratic culture: not just the extension of the right to vote to all adult men and women, but the widespread advent of popularly elected governments, and the expansion of welfare policies and of trade union influence. Working-class movements began to get at least a measure of their share of the seats of power. And because the voices of ordinary men and women now counted much more, the establishment began to take them seriously. By the 1950s, sociologists in the North were studying working-class culture in its own right, rather than simply seeing the poor as an aberration from, and threat to, "civilised" society. At the same time, historians increasingly recognised the partial nature of a discipline which concentrated on the elite and began to turn to labour history, to social history and to family history—and finally, with the women's movement, to women's history.

In many parts of the South, pressure from independence movements, combined with these shifts of attitude in the North, brought about the break-up of imperialism, and with it precisely the same shift of focus by historians from the colonial elite to the people of the newly independent nations. Independence, moreover, had often been preceded by a liberation struggle, ill-documented at the time, but now evidently crucial. The most recent countries to experience such a radical shift of focus are those of Southern Africa (see p43). *Mothers of the Revolution*, for example, presents the story of Zimbabwe's war of liberation "from the inside"—through the first-hand accounts of the women who kept their families, homes and villages going during the fighting [1].

Technological modernity and democratic inclusiveness are thus key characteristics of the oral history movement. It is now possible to capture the spoken word for the future, and transmit it across continents to vast audiences. In this, oral history has a power far beyond dry conventional historical writing, or the reports of statistical social surveys. It is one thing to read an academic study of Stalin; quite another to see and hear on television Russians recall their own lives as prisoners sent to the *gulag*, or as guards in the same camps.

Oral history and development

By tracing the growth of oral history practice in the North, we can see more clearly its relevance to development. Just as it helps to present a truer picture of the past by documenting the lives and feelings of all kinds of people otherwise hidden from history, so it can create a fuller understanding of the views and experience of the wide range of people too often excluded from the development debate. In addition, by allowing people to speak about any aspect of their lives, the oral history movement opened up vital new fields of enquiry—not just hidden voices but also hidden spheres of experience. Written documentation and official records always revealed more about the concerns of the political elite than those without political influence, about landowners rather than labourers, about men rather than women, about the educated rather than the illiterate, and about public rather than private life. Oral history offered new perspectives on many issues. It enabled people to examine welfare, for example, from the standpoint of those who receive it rather than those who give it out. It gave people the opportunity to talk about personal, social and cultural areas of experience. It revealed the connections between different spheres of activity, such as social and working life, and how, for example, working practices can influence patterns of family life.

A few other notable characteristics of oral history are especially relevant to development work. In the North, it has had a particular impact in the form of community history. This has been practised in a variety of ways, including recording old people for the publishing of local booklets, setting up tape archives, producing cassette tapes for use in schools, making radio programmes, and mounting travelling exhibitions.

The special quality in oral history which has encouraged this spread of community history is that it is fundamentally cooperative. It demands a wide range of skills, and is based on technologies—old and new—which are open to everyone, which makes it particularly suited to group work.

Oral history is also concerned with making connections between the older and younger generations, as has been most clearly shown in school projects. The most impressive educational work of this kind in the North has been the *Foxfire* project, which began in a small town high school in rural Georgia in the southern United States. The core to this was the interviewing of the older generation by the children, who then produced a magazine based largely on the interviews. The project caught the children's imagination and at the same time taught them skills for other purposes. But *Foxfire* also took off as a magazine and was soon selling well beyond the community: the magazine eventually became a best-selling book, and high schools all over the country have been trying to emulate it.

In a slightly more specialised way, oral history has been used in literacy work, both with children and adults. The clue to the success of this literacy work is closely connected with the essential nature of oral history. For it has been discovered that when people are listened to, they can gain new confidence that their experiences and their perceptions are worthwhile. This came as a surprise to the modern oral historians, who had simply set out to collect material for history. But they rather quickly discovered that most of those whom they recorded found the experience of telling their story a very positive one. Self-confidence is a key element in successful literacy teaching. By starting with the recording of the student's own life story, and then gradually transferring this into writing, the process of teaching can reinforce rather than undermine self-esteem. In Britain, where this technique has been widely used, there was for several years a magazine in which new learners could publish their work, called *Write First Time*, which gave further encouragement to the students.

Increased self-confidence is also the key to another branch of oral history work. This focuses on the elderly, especially those who live isolated lives, cut off from families and community— an increasingly common phenomenon in the North. This is known as "reminiscence work" and was pioneered by British oral historian Joanna Bornat for the NGO Help the Aged. By stimulating and developing the memories and recollections of old people, a sense of meaning and purpose in life can be rekindled, giving people who had become almost silent, something to relate and exchange with others [2].

Raising confidence, encouraging community action and cohesion, closing the gap between generations, providing the basis for literacy programmes, revitalising those marginalised by age or any other "disadvantage": all these qualities of oral history work can be applied to development practice.

Oral tradition

Wherever levels of literacy remain low, oral tradition continues to play a crucial social role in transmitting information, both about present custom and past practice. Mario Vargas Llosa's novel *The Storyteller* is a brilliant evocation of how, for a scattered group of Peruvian forest Indians on the upper Amazon, the elusive travelling *hablador*—as the missionaries called him—was the lifeline of a totally non-literate society on the edge of extinction [3]. Always on the move, he conveyed vital information of every type, from the most sacred religious truths to mere social gossip about distant neighbours.

In literate societies, too, oral tradition often remains important: in Africa, many communities have specialist narrators of local traditions. Their repertoire might include the genealogies of major families, records of land inheritance, and descriptions of major events such as battles, invasions, famines and drought. African oral tradition has been divided into five categories: learning formulas, rituals and slogans; lists of place names and personal names; official and private poetry— historical, religious or personal; stories—historical, didactic, artistic or personal; and legal and other commentaries [4].

Since the 1950s, a major school of African historical writing has developed which draws primarily on the recording and interpretation of oral tradition. Earlier colonial administrators and missionaries had recorded oral traditions, finding them both interesting and sometimes of practical value in understanding local beliefs; but historians had made no use of them, although the only written records normally at their disposal were those of the colonisers.

The pioneer of what is now a highly specialised historical technique, was Jan Vansina, a Belgian who worked in the Congo. His book *Oral Tradition*, revised as *Oral Tradition as History*, is the classic text on this method [5]. It has been used to trace the political history, migration movements, and agricultural and economic developments of African societies over long periods. Traditions are of course far from fixed; but in these historians' hands, changes and divergences between sources become evidence in themselves. In some of the most striking work, such as Steven Feierman's *The Shambaa Kingdom*, anthropology and social history are fused in an account of social change up to the present, which ranges from the material practicalities of daily living to the community's symbolic understanding of the universe [6].

Historians of Africa thus make important uses of such oral traditions. In Europe this practice is very rare: oral history is based almost entirely on direct memory and is a form of contemporary social history, constructed from personal accounts of life experience, public and private. Nevertheless, there are some social groups in Europe in whose culture oral traditions remain important. Some are surviving rural minorities, such as the mountain Protestants in France and Italy, or the Gaelic-speaking Scottish islanders who recall—as if they had witnessed them personally—the Highland clearances over 150 years ago, when they lost their lands to make way for sheep farms. More important for recent history, however, are the new generations of urban immigrants who have carried their traditions with them from the South, such as the Bengali seafarers from Sylhet, pioneer settlers of the Bangladeshi community in Britain [7].

Social research

The research activity of social scientists also overlaps with oral history, but whereas oral historians interview older people about the past, social scientists interview people to obtain documents for the interpretation of contemporary social change. Sometimes this is the same as oral history, sometimes not. Life story research in social science is now strongest in Europe—especially France and Germany—but the pioneers in both sociology and anthropology in the 1920s were in the United States. While British anthropologists, perhaps too influenced by the imperial manner, would sit under a sun umbrella communicating through an interpreter, and rarely used their informants' own words in their books, American anthropologists had already begun to publish full life story autobiographies from interviews with native Indians. This was the research approach used by Oscar Lewis for his famous studies of the culture of poverty in Mexico, such as *The Children of Sanchez* [8] and *Pedro Martinez* [9]. Latin America has a notably strong and socially committed tradition of life story research.

Finally, there is the closely related area of contemporary documentation in social research. This, too, can take the form either of in-depth interviewing, or of writing. While the immediate purpose is to understand what is happening now, the dimension of change, and so of the past, is rarely absent. And in the long run, such material can be as valuable for future historians as oral history or life story interviews. For example, in Britain the Mass Observation project was founded in 1937 to record the culture of ordinary people. Panels of diarists and essayists were recruited to record their everyday experiences and their work stored and catalogued: it is now a unique historical resource at the University of Sussex.

Focus on the future

This cluster of techniques, all closely related, differ in their emphasis—past or present, oral or written, personal or collective; they also have primary attachments to different disciplines. But from our point of view, to build on these distinctions would be unhelpful. Our concern is with how these various overlapping forms of "listening" can contribute to development, the primary focus of which is the future. All offer ways of documenting the currents of change, and of discovering the meaning of change and continuity in the lives of ordinary men and women: of coming closer to understanding their social consciousness and individual identity.

It is these awkwardly individual human lives, on which enduring development ultimately depends, which have too rarely informed development practice. Instead, this has been dominated by the views and ideas of the educated elite. Priorities have been largely dictated by those in control of financial and technical resources. But technology can now be used to narrow rather than widen the gap between "the haves and the have-nots": the tape recorder has opened up a means to capture and communicate the immense variety of individual experience, and so encourage development initiatives which more closely reflect the values and priorities of those they are meant to benefit.

CHAPTER THREE

FIRST PERSON

Putting people at the centre of development

The last 10 years have seen significant attempts by development academics and practitioners to transform the development process by insisting that it become more people-centred [1]. The wisdom of conventional experts and technocrats with their blueprints for economics, agriculture, education and health has been challenged and exposed as being out of touch with the needs and experience of the poor, and often obstructive to their real hopes for change. Participatory development is now seen as the best approach for achieving change, allowing people to become agents and not just objects of the development process.

The experience of NGOs and other development agencies, combined with the increasing amount of social science research now taking place in development, has confirmed the importance of taking account of the voice and experience of poor communities themselves if change is to be effective. Robert Chambers, of Britain's Institute of Development Studies in Sussex, has led the way in calling for "professional reversals", by which development workers become the listeners and learners, while those whose lives they intend to "develop" are increasingly recognised as the teachers and experts. At the heart of this reversal is the need for effective dialogue between the development establishment and the people who will be the agents of change, a dialogue that is likely to be primarily oral, and to feature a strong historical perspective.

Oral culture

A first step in any development dialogue, therefore, must be to acknowledge and respect the predominantly oral culture of many poor communities. An essentially oral culture will be unfamiliar to most development workers and researchers. Many will have been brought up in highly literate societies and will be used to testing and communicating their ideas on paper through the written word. Others may have become detached from the oral culture of their families by receiving formal, Western-influenced education.

Such people can find themselves strangely ill-informed in a society where the written word has less importance than the spoken word. They become the ignorant ones, with little access to the knowledge possessed by the community. And, just as oral cultures can be suspicious of the printed word, because it expresses power and law, so literacy breeds its own scepticism and suspicion about oral information and knowledge. The subjective and selective nature of memory, the power of community or personal myth, the different ways of estimating and recording time, quantity, distance and so on—all these fuel the tendency of the literate to devalue oral evidence.

Because of these factors, large parts of people's experience and expertise can—and often does—remain invisible to development workers, and untapped during development planning. Robert Rhoades has wryly observed how this invisibility surrounds the knowledge and innovations of the world's poor farmers, who "seldom record their accomplishments in writing, rarely write papers about their discoveries, and do not attach their names and patents to these discoveries [2]." All too often, the tendency in development circles remains the same: if it is not written, it is not heard or discussed.

If the voice of poor communities is to be heard more often, it will have to be predominantly through oral encounters and exchanges. A major part of participatory development and "professional reversals" therefore involves development workers adapting to oral communication and accepting its value. This is not as simple as it might seem. Many literate people lack the skills needed in an oral culture—skills like listening, asking, telling, using ritual expressions, memorising and handing on information by word of mouth alone. An international oracy campaign for development workers would be a useful complement to the world's many literacy programmes.

The historical dimension

Another central element of effective development dialogue is an understanding and appreciation of history and social change. Most poverty and inequality has a pattern and a history, and any improved future for a community must unfold from a knowledge of the strengths and weaknesses of its present and its past. Inequalities may have roots in a number of different factors—political, economic, environmental, cultural, personal—all of which have a historical dimension.

The greater part of any discussion about development focuses on change. A process of enquiry and description forms the first step, as communities recount and identify the nature of their poverty, and development workers try to understand it. A significant part of this exchange should involve analysis of the past. As interventions are identified and the project takes shape, a historical perspective continues to be required so that the impact of the project can be evaluated over time.

Oral testimony and development

There are a variety of ways in which people's testimony can be used practically and effectively in relief and development work. The rest of this chapter looks at different kinds of development activity in which the collection and interpretation of oral testimony has a part to play.

Reclaiming indigenous technical knowledge

People's technical knowledge and expertise about the environment in which they live—referred to as indigenous technical knowledge (ITK)—includes skills and practices in agriculture, health, botany, nutrition, arts, crafts, business and trading. Oral testimony projects can be used to discover the evolution of particular techniques and to uncover people's expertise and experience. Such investigations can help project workers gain an understanding of past experiments and innovations, and thus steer clear of re-invention. It also means that technical discussions can begin with everyone on an equal footing and avoids the situation where the extension worker persuades people to adopt practices they know to be inappropriate.

In India, the *Honey Bee* project collects the traditional

Documenting traditional knowledge and contemporary innovation

Honey Bee, an informal newsletter started in India in 1990, represents an attempt to collect and share the knowledge and skills of farmers and artisans, while avoiding the potential hazards of knowledge extraction. As well as documenting innovations, traditional practices and beliefs, it actively lobbies for the protection of the intellectual property rights of grassroots innovators, by creating pressure "so that anyone using farmers' knowledge will feel responsible for sharing the returns with the innovators in kind, cash or honor". Those involved have developed a database and are trying "to create controls within an international registration system so that innovations catalogued in the database are not available without the explicit permission of the trust registering these innovations [27]."

Honey Bee generates debate not only about sustainable alternatives based on people's knowledge systems, but also about the relationship between this and more formal systems. When the magazine invited comment on farmers' practices from veterinary and agricultural scientists, they judged quite a number of the practices "invalid". This provoked a spirited exchange of views.

Some members of the *Honey Bee* network felt that even the suggestion that validation by scientists was worthwhile implied a false superiority on the part of modern or Western science. Others queried the basis of the scientists' comments. When they labelled something as "needing verification", what kind of verification did they mean? If farmers find that something works, what further verification is necessary? When they consider something to be "unscientific", are scientists simply betraying the fact that they lack the appropriate framework through which to understand or explain traditional knowledge?

Editor Anil Gupta believes that dialogue between institutional scientists and farmer innovators is essential, while acknowledging that the relationship between the two systems is not always easy. The hope is that furthering the debate will enable some of the boundaries to be crossed and encourage the development of methodologies so that farmers and academics can work together to conduct experiments in the field. Gupta also hopes that *Honey Bee* will correct "the impression some people have that traditional knowledge is frozen in time and has to be resurrected in purely archival fashion", whereas such knowledge is not in fact static, but is continually evolving to suit changing conditions.

Honey Bee has a strong networking role, appealing to researchers, development workers, activists and farmers in many countries to identify and share local knowledge. In areas where the oral tradition is strong and remains an important means of generating and disseminating knowledge, farmers' practices and innovations can remain hidden from the "experts" unless they are prepared to take the time to listen. The term "resource-poor" farmers, often applied to those ekeing out a living from arid lands, is an indication of this deafness, for it is precisely those who manage to practise agriculture in an environment which defeats many modern attempts who can truly be regarded as resourceful. Indeed, the majority of the innovative practices documented by *Honey Bee* come from dry regions.

A further example of the value of breaking down the barriers between institutional and non-formal systems comes from West Africa where, after several major outbreaks of the Variegated Grasshopper devastated crops, extensive studies on the pest were undertaken. One strand of the work concentrated on farmers' knowledge: the researchers found that farmers were well aware of the insect's ecology (its relationship with the environment) and in certain cases made suggestions for control which anticipated the findings of the more conventional technical studies.

They concluded that the research of the outside scientists would have been "more useful and cost-effective if farmers' knowledge regarding grasshopper ecology had been considered from the outset. Instead, scientists apparently reconstructed information that was already available [from the farmers] and missed other data that the farmers could have provided." One of the most significant sources was the oral histories, which yielded much valuable information about the timing and severity of previous grasshopper attacks and the relative significance of damage to different crops [28].

knowledge and innovations of farmers and disseminates them through a magazine. The project has so far documented 500 innovative practices and applies scientific research to assess and develop them. In Bolivia, the Centro de Investigación y Promoción Educativa works with Aymara and Quechua people. It draws on elderly people's knowledge and experience to recover traditional Andean agricultural techniques and revive important social practices (see p26).

Research carried out by British agriculturalist Ken Wilson with elderly farmers, to construct an "environmental history" of Mazvihwa in Zimbabwe, uncovered a wealth of expert knowledge on land use and soil conservation [3]. Mazvihwa is an area of communal land in the dry southern part of Zimbabwe which was settled between 1920 and 1950 by people expelled from nearby ranches. It is a marginal arid area, not well suited to agricultural production and requiring great skill to farm. Interviews revealed detailed knowledge of the history and causes of soil erosion and many practical ideas about gulley control, contour ridges, ploughing patterns and land use which could minimise further erosion (see overleaf).

Wilson's research discovered that a substantial part of this local agricultural knowledge has been forced to remain idle in recent times, as successive government policies required people to settle and cultivate in ways that went against their better judgement. These policies have made farming an increasingly

The cost of no consultation

The arid marginal lands of the Mazvihwa region of Zimbabwe still bare the scars of the Rhodesian government's centralisation policy of the 1960s, when the authorities overrode traditional farming practices and ordered the deforestation and cultivation of previously untouched toplands. Local farmers, who were not consulted at the time but spoke their minds through an oral history project in the 1980s, recognised that this practice as well as other aspects of centralisation have greatly accelerated soil erosion in the region [29]. The new linear layout of housing settlements, for example, meant that the traditional system for the design and management of paths for people and cattle was abandoned. New paths had to fit in with the imposed centralised settlement patterns and even accommodate government Landrovers. They were seen as another major cause of the proliferation of gulleys and high degree of soil erosion, as a local farmer, Mr Chibidi, explained:

> In the old days paths were carefully laid out. They used to zig-zag. If one developed a gulley it would be moved. With centralisation, paths were defined between the fields...lots of people use them endlessly without changing them. Also people make their own short cuts without thinking.

Before centralisation, according to Mr Chikombeka, another farmer, careful soil conservation practices were followed:

> People had a lot of knowledge about this. They fenced their homes with gates that would direct the movement of people. If a road was bad it would be stopped. Cases over this could be brought to a court, it was a crime. In the 1950s people could still be fined for bad behaviour in regard to paths....If a gulley started, people avoided using that section of the path. They simply told people not to, cutting a branch of chitarara (gardenia spatulifolia), placing it across the old path. This tree has its laws. They then pegged logs in the incipient gulley and put in leaves to trap the sand so that grass would grow.

The so-called technical expertise of the government agriculturalists also contributed to the worsening soil erosion. Farmers disagreed with the government policy of controlling bush encroachment in the grazing areas. This "de-bushing" policy had existed since the 1930s and was based on the principle that fewer shrubs and trees would allow for more plentiful grass. It has continued to be actively encouraged by government extension workers. However, the local farmers have always recognised that more grass and less bush results in more soil erosion and fewer woodland products. The government's introduction of ox-ploughing to replace intensive hoe cultivation is equally regretted by the Mazvihwa farming community. It has been another factor changing the way in which soil and water behave in the watershed and has made for faster and more concentrated patterns, as Mr Magwidi described:

> Water used to be scattered in the landscape; now it is concentrated and flows to the rivers...When you plough across a slope it leads to water collecting at one place, and when it gets an outlet it will do so with great force.

The oral history interviews recorded during this research gave farmers a chance to explain their knowledge and recount the history of agricultural mismanagement in their area. Much of their testimony was verified by extensive aerial photographs of Mazvihwa in 1939. These show that conditions in the watershed then were not as bad as they are today and provide evidence of the effectiveness of the previous systems of land management. The farmers' oral testimony also shows how local people's farming experience and expertise—their indigenous technical knowledge—can so often remain unheard and be overridden by centralised policy and planning, in this case for several decades.

risky business and greatly accelerated the rate of environmental degradation in the area.

The farmers' main complaint focused on the Rhodesian government's "centralisation" policy of the 1960s which had forced them to live in villages laid out in straight lines and allowed them to farm only certain parts of any watershed. They described how they had previously always farmed the fertile riverine areas of the watersheds and left the toplands as forest and bush. The government reversed this practice, outlawing the farming of alluvial soils along the rivers and ordering the deforestation and cultivation of the toplands. The memory of this experience is bitter. One farmer, Mr Chikombeka, graphically explained how soil erosion had worsened with the farming of the toplands:

> *If I fall from where I am sitting now, I won't hurt myself. But if I fall from the top of my house I will be bruised. Just the same is the effect of making people farm far from the rivers: the run-off builds up and has got power to erode, carrying a lot of soil.*

The farmers' views were presented in a report to key policy makers in Zimbabwe's Ministry of Lands, Agriculture and Resettlement, with much of the oral testimony quoted verbatim. The report generated an unusually high level of response from the ministry staff. As their comments indicated, they were particularly struck by reading the words of the farmers themselves: "For me the highlight of the paper is the extremely perceptive comments from the informants"; and "It confirms that people who live on and by the land know a great deal more about their environment than do classroom technocrats like me." This study is a good example of how a collection of authoritative oral testimony, well presented, can

Reclaiming past skills

In the harsh climate and tough conditions of Bolivia's *altiplano*, men and women in their 40s are the elderly of their communities. The high altitude, freezing winters and poor soils combined with malnutrition and a lack of basic services all contribute to a low life expectancy (55.4 years for women and 51 for men). Yet, despite the closeness of generations, traditional knowledge and practices are fast disappearing.

In the northern region of the department of Potosí, one of the poorest and most isolated in Bolivia, a severe drought in the 1980s caused irreparable damage to the *altiplano*, as springs and rivers ran dry, soils were eroded and traditional grazing lands, along with the native plants and animals, gradually receded. The consequent loss of productive land dramatically increased the practice of male migration, leaving the elderly and mothers and children to scratch a living from the inhospitable surroundings on their own.

The Aymara were the original inhabitants of the region and although they have gradually integrated with the Quechua, their social and political systems—the *ayllus*—have survived. Essentially the *ayllus* is an area of land (with no clearly defined boundary) encompassing a number of communities bound together by common local government, judicial and educational systems, as well as by ritual and spiritual custom. But worsening economic conditions are now eroding the old patterns of life, one consequence of which is the increasing marginalisation of the old, and the vulnerable, such as widows and orphans. With support from HelpAge International, the Centro de Investigación y Promoción Educativa (CIPE) is working with these communities to recover some of the practices of mutual support and solidarity and to involve the elderly in activities which will both raise awareness of and enhance their contributions to their community's future development.

All CIPE workers in this project originate from the *altiplano* themselves, speak the local languages and are familiar with the *ayllu*. With the agreement of the *ayllu* assemblies, parts of the common land have been ceded for the use of the fitter older people, and their traditional ways of planting, fertilising and irrigating open land have been documented by CIPE agricultural technicians. While the soils have undoubtedly deteriorated over the years, the customary cultivation techniques—which rely on intimate knowledge of a fragile ecosystem rather than on technology and chemical inputs—may offer a more economic and sustainable level of productivity. With the communities' help, CIPE workers have also recorded details of all the medicinal plants in the area, as well as their uses.

The knowledge of the elderly is being actively sought in other ways. Many of the older women have taken up the invitation to demonstrate how garments, belts and bags are woven in the beautiful traditional designs which were fast being forgotten. Older people are also sharing their memories of daily life in the *altiplano*, which are now being systematically recorded. In a rapidly changing society, adversely affected by increasing poverty and migration, the individual and collective experiences of life in the past which are emerging may help to regenerate community solidarity and pride. The *ayllus* was an advanced system of social organisation, with the traditions and the power to protect the most vulnerable. If some of the original survival mechanisms can be revived and adapted, recollections of the past will have actively contributed to the region's future development.

catch the attention of those in power. It shows how compelling the words of real people can be. It is not easy to leave such words buried in an in-tray. They demand an answer and tend to haunt even the most hardened bureaucrat.

Disaster relief

Oral histories have proved particularly useful as a means of understanding the ways in which people cope with the kind of recurrent disasters such as drought, famine, flood and displacement which affect many millions of people. In such situations, people often make decisions according to precedent. Many communities, for whom these disasters are part of life, have a certain kind of crisis history which it is in their interest to pass on from generation to generation and to take account of in their decision-making. People fleeing conflict, for example, will seek refuge in areas which have welcomed them before or where they have some connections. People coping with drought or famine will utilise strategies for procuring food or grazing which have proved effective in the past. An understanding of this crisis history becomes equally important for relief and development workers if their programmes of assistance are to be truly supportive of people's customary coping strategies. Conducting interviews is one important way of finding out about these histories, but another source is oral artistry. Times of disaster become part of the collective memory and often gather around them a large body of songs, stories, legends and proverbs. These, too, can be drawn upon to understand events and piece together precedent.

Drought and famine

One example of the way in which a knowledge of history and precedent is critical to people's survival strategies comes from the Gabbra pastoralists. It demonstrates how important "historical competence" is in the struggle for a livelihood in the rangelands around the border between Kenya and Ethiopia [4]. Gabbra herdsmen are acutely aware of historical cycles which determine climatic conditions in the area. Years are named in cycles of seven, like days of the week, and the elders remember precise weather patterns for each year as far back as 80 years. By referring to this historical calendar they believe they can identify weather cycles, and predict the weather for each coming year and so move their herds accordingly, as they or their fathers did in the last similar cycle. The Gabbra also have a detailed knowledge of genealogies within the tribe, which record kinship patterns and obligations. Genealogy and descent affect marital relations, the rights to residence and the sharing of pasture and livestock. Paul Robinson, who researched and documented the Gabbra calendar and cyclical view of life, believes their oral rainfall data is extremely accurate when compared with scientific data, and observed: "A correct interpretation of climatic history, together with a thorough knowledge of genealogical history and the linkages for assistance that genealogy can provide, can...give a man and his dependents a significant edge in all matters of livestock management."

Oral history research in Malawi and Sudan has played an important part in learning more about people's experience of famine and their strategies for coping with it. During the 1980s in Malawi, Megan Vaughan used oral history interviews to delve back some 30 years and piece together the events of the 1949 famine. The findings drew attention to the need to recognise the role of gender as an important variable in famine relief policies [5]. The interviews provided a wealth of personal detail about the *ubombo*, or social breakdown, of family and community obligations to share food and income. In particular, they revealed the extreme vulnerability of women during the famine and their problems in gaining access to government relief.

Vaughan's study is also a good example of how songs can be a particularly fruitful source of oral testimony. She collected women's songs, sung while pounding grain, which date from the time of the famine and are still in common use. In the book which resulted, she uses the songs alongside the interviews she conducted, some 105 in total, to provide a particularly female perspective on the famine. The interviews and songs both show how the structure of society worked against women during the famine: it was both matrilocal (when the husband goes to live with the wife's group) and matrilineal (based on the female line of ancestors). Because of their childcare responsibilities and their position as owners and cultivators of land, women were tied to their villages and were unable to make full use of the wider variety of coping strategies available to men.

Furthermore, because of the matrilineal system, many men did not feel a strong sense of obligation to their wives and families. When they migrated they often failed to return, or to send food or cash. Ironically, the colonial government would not recognise the women as family heads, and were tragically slow to register them for relief. As a result, as the songs and testimony reveal, women, their children and the elderly were particularly isolated and were the most harshly affected by the famine.

A number of pounding songs capture the marital tensions of the famine days. One shows how strong the social pressure was for men to migrate to support their families:

> *What type of husband are you*
> *Staying at home with the women?*
> *The other men are off to Mwenza now*
> *Why not you?*
> *You just stay here and your only 'work'*
> *Is to fondle women.*

Another song sums up women's feelings of abandonment when men did migrate but then did not meet their obligations. So many men failed to return that 1949 became known as "the year of divorces":

> *We have suffered this year*
> *Our men are divorcing us.*
> *Oh, what shall we do with this hunger?*

Other songs record how women were then forced to resort to desperate measures and abnormal behaviour in order to survive. Some were themselves forced to migrate, and become prostitutes in the cities for the price of a meal:

> *I must go to Limbe*
> *And board a bus,*
> *My body will pay for the fare.*
> *In Lilongwe my body will do,*
> *In Limbe it will do,*
> *In Blantyre it will do,*
> *And in Salisbury it will do.*

Other women had no choice but to abandon the youngest children and the very old, leaving them without food to save themselves and their other children. The women's songs complement people's accounts, illustrating vividly the fact that men had a greater number of survival strategies open to them and underlining the role of gender and marital relations in "shaping" disaster and creating "a pattern of suffering".

Similar oral history research by Alex de Waal into the 1985 famine in the Darfur region of Sudan involved 150 individual and group interviews in eight villages, one area on the urban outskirts and one famine camp [6]. Among other things, the testimony gathered by de Waal showed how people's naming of particular events can often highlight key issues and provide a fertile starting point for further discussion and learning. In naming previous famines, people in Darfur were distinguishing between types of famine, and when they explained what the names meant, they effectively described and categorised a wide range of famine experience.

Like the Malawi study, de Waal's research aimed "to analyse famine from the perspective of the rural people who suffered it" and to encourage relief agencies "to listen to, debate with, and understand people who suffer famine...who are, after all, the proven experts at surviving famines". Listening to the history of famine in Darfur from the late nineteenth century onwards revealed people's current understanding of and reactions to famine. It soon became obvious that "hunger is only one manner of suffering". The varied character and severity of different famines and the particular kinds of suffering they engender are lost in the single English word "famine", which has dominated and perhaps obscured relief workers' and donor agencies' perceptions of the subject.

Relatively mild famines in Darfur, characterised mainly by food shortages and very high grain prices, were given names such as *Um Goldi*, which refers to the small measure of grain available in a Goldi cigarette packet, or *Abu Arobein* (the father of 40), which refers to the large number of *piastres* (coins) required to buy a single measure of grain. When conditions were more severe and people were forced to resort to the despised practice of eating wild foods, famines were given names such as *Um Mukheita*, the mother of *mukheita*, a berry gathered and eaten in times of distress. The names of more severe famines refer to the kind of disaster when more important social conventions were violated. The great eighteenth century famine is remembered as *Karo Tindel* (eating bones) and that of 1913-14 is called *Ab Jildai* (father of the skins). Both names recall a time when people resorted to the shameful practice of eating animal carcasses rather than ritually slaughtered meat.

Equally direct are the names which commemorate and define the worst of all possible types of famine, when the community breaks down and disperses, and people become destitute and displaced. One such famine is known as *Julu* (the wandering) and another as *Nitlaaga* (we'll meet again). Others are more explicit still. *Um Sudur* (mother of the chest) refers to a time when people crawled upon their chests in desperation and suffering, and the great famine of 1949 is remembered as *Um Regeba* (mother of the knees), to mark another period when people were reduced to crawling and despair. The famine of 1984-85 is known as *Ifza'una* which means "save us" and speaks of utter helplessness. It is also remembered as "Reagan", after the American relief food that eventually arrived in the region.

This "hierarchy of names" and the way these experiences were described and differentiated show that the major focus of concern about famine for the people of Darfur was not that it can cause hunger or even death, but that it can bring destitution, destroy individual livelihoods and break down their society. People's testimony confirmed that coping strategies in the 1985 famine were aimed primarily at avoiding destitution rather than simply staving off hunger. Their accounts showed that survival strategies were sophisticated and often involved levels of "planned hardship", with the priority being the preservation of their way of life at all costs. Such planning involved saving seed, staying on hand to plant, and managing elaborate grazing strategies to preserve herds.

Clearly, what people were trying to do was much more complex than food-aid agencies supposed. The oral testimonies showed up important discrepancies between people's strategies and those of relief agencies. The wider understanding which resulted has consequently stimulated debate about how famine relief can be made more appropriate, going beyond food-aid interventions to include other supportive measures concerned with the survival of herds, the continued functioning of market mechanisms, preparation for future harvests and the prevention of destitution and dispersal.

War, displacement and refugees

Oral histories have also proved useful in throwing light on the repercussions of war and the social consequences of displacement. In Mozambique, Jovito Nunes used oral history to trace the fortunes of two displaced groups in Zambezia: the Tacuane-speaking people from Namanjavira and the Nyo-speaking people from Eururuni [7]. Both groups were displaced by the civil war and forced to settle around the town of Mocuba for several years between 1981 and 1991. In oral history interviews collected by Nunes in 1992, people described the intricate social and economic changes that occurred within their societies when they took refuge amongst neighbouring people (see overleaf). Their stories told not only of the struggle for survival but also of the price paid for that survival. The narratives make clear that these people knew what they needed to make their survival easier and were of course best placed to design their own relief programmes—but this was not to be.

Oral testimony collection like Nunes' work contributes to an increasing recognition of the variety of refugee experience. Instead of all displaced people being given the same "package" of support, more appropriately targeted interventions should be developed which build on a community's strengths and minimise their particular vulnerabilities. Listening to the experience and expertise of refugees themselves reveals many more options for relief agencies working with the displaced. Aid agency support of historically or economically based strategies of self-settlement and survival, like those of the Nyo people, may be a better response than the provision of set-piece alternatives such as camps and relief aid. The first step in such a process is the opportunity for each community to describe their situation and voice their particular needs and priorities. In the case of the Tacuane and Nyo peoples, this happened too late in their period of displacement. Much more can be done for refugees and the displaced if they are listened to earlier.

Factual history is not the only clue to people's strategies in times of disaster. Stories collected from the Dinka in southern Sudan, by British anthropologist and relief worker John Ryle, show how the legends and tales which people tell about disasters can reveal a great deal about their experience and strategies during such events [8]. The stories told during the war and famine which affected the Dinka people in 1988 illustrate the significance of a certain kind of storytelling in a time of extreme crisis: they set out the Dinka's priorities for survival and also acted as a source of encouragement.

Ryle recounts how Wek Agoth, the chief of the Aguok, described the impact of the 1988 war and famine by drawing on stories of the great disaster which befell his people in the Mahdiyya period of the 1890s, and also on some of the Dinka creation myths. The stories seemed to stress the importance of saving a way of life and preserving the future of the group, over and above saving individuals. They showed that Dinka notions of survival were different from those of the relief agencies and this insight became key to understanding the actions and reactions of the Dinka during the famine. Furthermore, the stories themselves expressed firm hope for the future and looked beyond the apparent hopelessness of famine and war. They were exchanged between people and sustained them in a way which made one Dinka, Joseph Malual, remark that "stories are also a kind of food", highlighting how stories and legends not only provide important technical information about precedent and strategy in a disaster, but are of equivalent spiritual value to a community in crisis.

Family tracing

Oral histories are frequently collected in the family tracing and reunification programmes which often take place in the aftermath of war or large-scale disasters. Wives, husbands and children are separated; people are left destitute and out of touch with their place of origin and extended family. The accurate compilation of personal histories helps to uncover people's particular journeys, mapping out the itinerary of their displacement and collecting information about their homes and family members. This information is then transcribed and sent to other refugee centres or villages to be cross-checked with the accounts of other separated persons.

A memorial to the largest example of this kind of tracing programme is in the museum of the International Committee of the Red Cross (ICRC) in Geneva. The case histories of the millions of prisoners and refugees separated from their families in the Second World War are kept there on display. Each file tells its own tale of misery and separation. Some, but not all, tell of eventual family tracing and reunification. ICRC's attempts to

Displacement and survival strategies

An oral history project with two displaced communities in Mozambique revealed how their different characteristics helped and hindered adaptation to changed circumstances [30].

The largest recorded movement of Tacuane-speaking people took place in 1986, when 13,000 fled to Mocuba, Mozambique, after a major RENAMO attack. Their testimonies contain graphic descriptions of killing, flight and separation. On arrival they were given shelter in government centres and emergency aid which lasted for two years. During this time, relations between the displaced and the host community deteriorated: "[The host community] hated us because we received food and clothes," said Favor Mario.

But when official aid stopped, things went from bad to worse as the displaced people inevitably became dependent on the local community. Their land allocations were too small to allow self-sufficiency and they were forced to work as *ganyo-ganyo* (agricultural labourers), often neglecting their own fields. They were soon totally dependent on the original inhabitants, who paid them in grain or clothes. Armindo Evazungo, one of the Tacuane-speaking people, describes this vicious cycle:

> *Doing ganyo-ganyo this year means doing it next year and the following year and so on. If, for example, your wife is going to do ganyo-ganyo that means that you won't have enough people working on the family farm. This means that you won't harvest very much and you will soon run out of your food reserve. You will always be begging.*

This virtual slave labour took on a new and damaging dimension when the host community demanded that women only should work the fields. This division of labour was unprecedented in Tacuane culture and was made worse by the fact that the employers only paid them in women's clothes. Women suddenly had control of the resources in the household. Deep feelings of animosity gradually developed: men felt marginalised and powerless while women felt overworked and unsupported. Vineza Sabonete expressed the women's point of view:

> *Men are becoming boring fellows these days. They behave like children just because we do not bring them trousers. We are not supposed to sustain men; they are supposed to sustain us. Look, I do ganyo-ganyo and I gain some clothes. Sometimes I wear them myself or give them to the girls. I also made sheets out of them for us and for the children. Besides, who brings vegetables home? Me, not him. So he should thank me for that.*

Men's feelings of resentment and powerlessness increased and were reflected in a collapse of social and sexual mores and a rise in insulting behaviour. With so many families split up by the civil war, many women lacked uncles, fathers and husbands to protect them and help resolve conflict. At the same time, the need for kinship support and arbitration grew as men's harassment of women increased. Flore Nhanala explains:

> *In our home area each man had his spear and nobody would dare to harass a woman if they knew she was the wife, daughter or niece of such and such...but*

here most of us do not have relatives and men are different. We have stopped talking to them about what they do. There is no point in talking to them. They start to drink. They bring us troubles because they have to cheat someone to get the drink. They insult us. We don't talk any more...this is war. If this war ended we could go back and they could work as they always did.

The Nyo-speaking people were displaced more gradually between 1981 and 1985, until 10,000 of them were living in the cramped *bairro* on the outskirts of Mocuba. Their community survived much better than that of the Tacuane people by virtue of a more entrepreneurial strategy. Their social and economic history had been more varied and they had a tradition of migrant labour. This gave their community an important "elasticity" which allowed them to continue trading and to adapt to separation and dispersal. They gravitated naturally towards other migrant labourers and traders, settled themselves in this community and so were not reliant on government assistance. Jovito Nunes, who collected the interviews, notes that people spoke of a strong "ideology of mutual help", which was typical of migrant labourers. The Nyo-speaking people were soon integrated into business and trading networks, working in thatching, brick-making, and selling dried fish and maize on the black market. Families also often separated by choice: husbands would do business in the *bairro* while women cultivated land they had been given. Ernesto Nanguachinua explained the system:

When I came here I didn't know anybody. I was given shelter by a family I didn't know. I worked for them for some time. I went to the fields with them in Namagoa. They also had a business here in Mocuba, selling cigarettes, dried fish, cooking oil and so on...I had to be patient. I learned the channels, how to get things and where to sell them. I got on well with the head of the household and he gave me a plot of land. Most of them have huge plots of land in Namagoa which they don't cultivate, but they won't give them to you unless they trust you. To have these plots for yourself is very helpful because you have two homes. Now because of war we consider our main home to be here....In Namagoa we have just a small hut for our wives and children to sleep in during the week while we do business here. In October, November and December we go there to help them because it is the height of the agricultural season. But when they hear about a possible RENAMO attack they [wives and children] run away and come back here.

This support system worked both ways, as Primo Manual explained:

If you live in a community like this where you don't have your real family you must be clever. You must help others so that they can help you when you are in need.....If I had no friends or contacts in this area I would get stuck....A true man must move around here; you can't just expect these things will come to you.

This kind of research into patterns of flight and survival shows the importance, if effective support is to be given, of understanding people's particular asylum strategies, which have often been developed over time and draw on established contacts and practices.

unite families continue in many parts of the world to this day. The social welfare ministries of an increasing number of African governments have also developed tracing and reunification programmes in recent years, to deal with large numbers of families separated as a result of years of civil war [9]. Countries such as Mozambique, Angola, Liberia, Uganda and Ethiopia all have programmes in which social workers collect the life stories and oral testimony of children and adults, in an attempt to establish their identity and trace their remaining family members. Much of this work is with children and involves particularly sensitive interviewing work (see Chapter Four, p73).

Cultural preservation and consciousness-raising

Effective development action often requires a sense of common identity and purpose, which is difficult to generate when people have become detached from or lost a sense of their cultural roots: their history, values, and social and political structures. A weak cultural identity can make a community more vulnerable to the imposition of development schemes which may be inappropriate. And development which does not reflect the values and culture of a society is unlikely to be sustainable.

Throughout the world, traditional communities are increasingly fragmented and undermined, particularly in rural areas. This may be as a result of "westernisation" through the media and educational systems, urbanisation and industrialisation, or because of more violent ethnic conflict, political repression or neglect, or economic pressures leading to migration. In some cases it is a question of life and death: some indigenous peoples are in danger of extinction. Others, such as the Innu in Canada, hunters and gatherers forced to settle in grim villages in the 1950s when their lands were taken up with large-scale industrial development, feel so morally and emotionally damaged by having to give up much of their way of life, that many feel their existence has lost its meaning. In the words of Rose Gregoire, an Innu social worker:

> *I always think about my mother, I think, "Why didn't I learn the traditional things from her?" Today I can't make moccasins, I can't make anything....I feel so depressed at times, I really don't*

know what to think. Sometimes I feel my lifestyle was robbed from me. And then you tend to think you are nothing, not a person and not an Innu [10].

Reclaiming traditions, culture and language plays a crucial part in rebuilding a common consciousness and sense of dignity and purpose for people who have endured inequalities or oppression of some kind. Allowing people to speak for themselves in their own words has a key role to play in this process.

In 1992, the Innu, only too aware of how their society was in a downward spiral of unemployment, alcoholism and family neglect, were shocked into action by the deaths of six children in a house fire while their parents drank. They decided to hold a People's Enquiry to look back at the last 30 years, to encourage people to talk about their problems and start to express their hopes and regain control over the future. The result was a bilingual book called *Gathering Voices: Finding strength to help our children*, which contained analysis, drawings, photographs, stories, poems and the words of some 142 elders, adults and children. The introduction states:

Our history has always been told to us through stories from our parents and grandparents. This gathering of voices tells the history of our people at this point in time. We see this...as a tool to help us solve our problems, on our road to recovery...an important building block in our future discussions towards self-government [11].

A key part of the Innu's determined effort to overcome their problems was to regain a sense of history and pride in their traditions: "Our elders drink too much...because we don't care and we don't listen to them. We don't hear them because we drink too much, and we don't look after our children"; "We can't blame all our problems on alcohol. We have to blame ourselves too, for not taking care of the caribou bones"; and "We don't respect the animal spirits...we are losing our traditions....We should get our culture and traditions back [12]."

Oral testimony projects like this can help to mobilise a culture under threat, encouraging the revival of some traditions and conveying them to current and future generations as well as to outsiders. This, in turn, serves to define community identity more clearly and boost confidence. In many such projects, the process of reclaiming tradition is combined with an active educational function. Stories, songs, histories and technical knowledge which have been gathered in this way can be put to creative use within school curricula, adult literacy projects or in health education programmes.

In the Caribbean, oral history projects of this kind—including a network of "memory banks"—are a practical and increasingly common reaction to the cultural colonialism which is felt to be destroying Caribbean culture and obscuring the region's history and identity (see p40). All the projects have a strong inter-generational emphasis and a commitment to a dynamic rather than purely archival form of documentation and presentation. Their goal is to preserve the memories and experiences of the older generations who hold so much of the past in their heads, but also to communicate Caribbean history and tradition to the young. This is seen as an urgent priority if Caribbean identity is to be affirmed and people are to seek out an alternative path to development which embraces rather than ignores or rejects Caribbean traditions.

The Folk Research Centre in St Lucia aims to preserve and promote the country's cultural heritage so that young people and their communities can begin to ask what kind of a future

Culture for development

While their oral testimony project was based on the concept of the Jamaica Memory Bank (see overleaf), the Folk Research Centre (FRC) of St Lucia was clear from the start that its aim was more than cultural preservation alone. One of its explicit objectives is "to explore and clarify the role of culture in the development of our people". As the last generations who hold the details of traditional customs and technology and forms of social organisation gradually die, and as other cultural mores become ever more influential, especially since the advent of satellite TV, there is a growing urgency to document the country's cultural resources. The Centre's purpose is not simply preservation of the past, but analysis of the material for its relevance to modern development strategies. This reflects a strong feeling that current development action is ignoring or even impoverishing many sections of the community and that alternative methods and forms of social organisation are needed.

The training for the interviewers, mainly history students and graduates, includes an explanation of the scope of the Centre's work, and the oral history project; introduces the concept of the Memory Bank, linked to examples of completed field work; and focuses on the history of St Lucia, in particular the Kwéyòl culture. Interviewers are familiarised with Kwéyòl forms of expression, especially the way people tend to define time and the use and significance of certain recurrent phrases.

The interviews, recorded on audio cassettes, are analysed for the information they yield on traditional culture and technology, social life and history. Photographs and printed materials are also collected. The FRC's aim is then to feed this information back into as wide a cross-section of the community as possible, to solicit their response to the material and incorporate any suggestions into the future work of the project. This is being done through community workshops, which include a photo exhibition (featuring some of the interviewees) and a slide presentation on aspects of St Lucia's culture, and a more "formal" presentation of the project's findings—in Kwéyòl—by a well-known member of the local community, followed by a piece of theatre based on the stories collected. People then have the chance to comment and respond, and in the afternoon to join in various entertainments and activities run by local cultural groups.

---

they want (see above). Recent years have seen an onslaught of imported models of popular culture via satellite TV and commercialism, mostly from America. Foreign influence has also been strong in designing educational curricula, and the local Creole language is gradually being eroded. The Centre trains and employs elders to collect life stories and local knowledge and then makes up "culture-kits" for schools which contain tapes, artefacts, photographs and written materials which can be used in a variety of cross-curriculum activities.

The role of collective culture and personal memory is especially important in maintaining a sense of identity and

Memory banks

"An old man dies...a book is lost"

This African saying has particular poignancy in the Caribbean region, where so much of the cultural heritage, particularly the African, is unrecorded. In 1981, in an attempt to rescue a whole "library" of knowledge and skills, the Jamaica Memory Bank was established. It aimed to document the country's heritage "by tapping the memories of our Senior Citizens so that their knowledge can be available for posterity". The project was the initiative of a small group of people, whose pioneering work in the social sciences and documentation of folk music had alerted them to the rate at which Jamaica's traditional knowledge and culture were disappearing. The Memory Bank was soon supported by a much larger island-wide team, and by 1984 the project had inspired a regional seminar, which resulted in the setting up of a network of memory banks throughout the Caribbean.

In this region a key factor in the waning of traditional culture and history is the influence of mass media, which bring North American entertainment and values right into people's homes. But more importantly, many Caribbean people are descendants of African slaves, who were actively discouraged from continuing their cultural practices. In some cases this policy was pursued so vehemently that it resulted in generations that had lost, and sometimes even rejected, African-based lifestyles or practices. The descendants of Indian plantation workers, who had more cultural freedom, have retained a relatively strong sense of identity and history. The Jamaica Memory Bank has therefore focused particularly on the Afro-Caribbean heritage.

The project is organised on a parish basis. Each of the island's 14 parishes has a coordinator, and the interviewing is carried out by a network of volunteers, trained by a team of professional researchers. Materials collected in the field range from tape-recorded interviews to videos, artefacts, photographs and manuscripts. After a copy has been taken for the Memory Bank, the original interview cassette is stored in the National Library in Kingston. Subject to copyright agreements and any confidentiality safeguards, this tape becomes available to the public.

The interviews range from single-topic discussions to whole life stories. By 1986 some 80 elderly Jamaicans had been interviewed. Seventy per cent were over 80 and 25% of those were 100 or older; about 20% of those interviewed had died by 1986. In addition to the interviews, about 1,500 songs had been taped, and ceremonies, celebrations and other activities of about 20 groups had been photographed, taped or filmed.

The material at the Memory Bank is carefully documented and analysed for the information it contains, for example, cultural, practical, scientific, botanical, linguistic or medical. Indexing and classifying such wide-ranging material has proved complicated, and the fact that the end uses vary makes the task even more difficult—the needs of a development practitioner, an academic researcher, a tourist organisation, the mass media, a lay person or a teacher are all different. Cross-referencing, while seen as essential, is also time-consuming, since a life story may contain brief but illuminating references to multiple topics.

In 1990 and 1993, as part of an expansion of activities and a focus on the research aspect, the Memory Bank got funding from HelpAge International specifically to provide interviewing equipment and training to older people (see p86). The aim was to involve them more in the running of the project, but it was also felt that the increased reciprocity of elder interviewing elder would generate easier conversation and more informative material. And their own knowledge of the past and the locality would help in the field research.

While the Memory Bank has a clear archival role, it was also conceived as having an important developmental function. As the pace of change increases and the economic and cultural influence of North America becomes ever more difficult to resist, it was felt that a stronger sense of Caribbean history would help the region define and pursue its own course of development: "In this region where so much relating to the lives and thinking of the people has been written from the observer's rather than the insider's point of view, a project such as the Memory Bank could redress the balance [31]."

purpose among involuntary migrants and refugees coming to terms with exile and isolation. The United Nations Convention Relating to the Status of Refugees (1951) declares the "maintenance of culture" as a particular right of refugees. In these communities the elderly, traditionally an important repository for a people's culture, are often especially marginalised. Uprooted to unfamiliar surroundings, they no longer have the customary authority which comes with land ownership, property, local knowledge and advanced years. In the desperate scramble to understand a new situation, the knowledge and social standing of the elderly can be devalued, while the younger generations try to master their new environment and increasingly lose touch with the old one.

Roddy Mupedziswa, a Zimbabwean social worker, has observed how in Mozambican refugee camps in Zimbabwe, the social status of the elderly has declined significantly. He notes that one important consequence of this decline in social status is the deterioration in communication between the generations, particularly between the very old and the youth of the refugee community [13]. These young people have grown up seeing their elderly relatives with little obvious role to play. They have also grown up without detailed knowledge of "home".

The HelpAge refugee programme in Zimbabwe has increasingly encouraged the use of oral history and the regeneration of oral artistry such as songs and stories. Various cultural projects have attempted to put elderly people back at the centre of the refugee community's cultural and social life, and deliberately brought young and old together through storytelling, song and dance. This has given elderly people a new official forum in which to pass on cultural information and good counsel to the younger generation. The aim was to reinstate elderly people at the social heart of the refugee community, while also preserving and documenting group history and culture for the next generation.

Similar cultural preservation and education projects are operating inside countries where rapid change is threatening people's sense of identity and where the predominantly Western models of education are seen as inappropriate or failing to meet the needs of poor people. In such situations, the incorporation of traditional oral material into the curriculum can introduce more accessible and relevant teaching resources, as well as providing some sense of stability and continuity in periods of change and transition. Educational materials are usually expensive and often in short supply in schools, libraries and bookshops in many parts of the South; the development of local materials can provide more resources—and more culturally appropriate ones—at lower cost.

In Sierra Leone, the Stories and Songs Project of the People's Educational Association, collects traditional songs and stories which it tape records and transcribes for use in its own and other organisations' adult education programmes [14]. The project has so far published 40 collections of stories and songs—a valuable contribution both to the volume and style of local literacy resources.

The need for indigenous educational material also becomes acute as people emerge from repression and dictatorial regimes where educational resources have been heavily censored or prescribed. In South Africa, the Church group *Eyethu Imbali* (Xhosa for "Our History") collects people's life stories and uses them to produce material for the 10- to 17-year-old age group. This provides them with alternative reading material, and introduces them to a new and different kind of history from that which they are taught at school.

Oral history and the preservation of the nation's oral literature has similarly emerged as a vital, if controversial, development issue in Namibia since its independence. The task of recovering Namibia's history from colonial bias is seen as a

Namibian oral history: a question of politics

Because oral testimony can empower people—minorities, special interest groups, individuals—it can become an intensely political and politicised activity.

Before independence, the history of Namibia was very largely written by white South African and German historians and a scattering of European missionary and traveller "eye-witnesses". But this emphasis on colonial and missionary records has inevitably led to a Eurocentric, indeed imperialist, slant. Since independence there has been a growing movement among Namibians to redress the balance and record indigenous versions of Namibian history. The result has been the ambitious—and controversial—Namibian Orature Project (NOP), where "orature" encompasses oral history, literature and tradition.

The NOP has run into difficulties. It has discovered that there are competing versions of oral "evidence" that undermine the search for collective Namibian history. A vivid example is the life of the Herero leader, Samuel Maharero, who was both a resistance hero and pragmatic political leader. The only full, published life of Maharero, by a South African professor drawing largely on archival sources, has been condemned as a travesty, slanderous and factually wrong, by many Herero *savants*—keepers of oral tradition. Of particular concern to the *savants*, quite apart from errors in lineage, were the aspersions cast on Maharero's courage and sobriety, largely based on written German sources.

An attempt by the Herero Cultural Council, representing one of the principal tribal groups in Namibia, to collect their own version of Herero history, including the life of Maharero, ran into opposition from the minority Mbanderu people. The Mbanderu share Herero ancestry and do not accept that the Herero Council can speak for all Herero Mbanderu people. Another problem has been the political agenda. The different political parties are seeking Herero votes. They want to establish, in their favour, their place in the struggle for independence. Each party views the oral history of their opponents with suspicion. Add to this the concerns of other major groups, such as the Hereros' traditional rivals the Nama, that the Herero oral history project was attempting to place Herero history at the top of a hierarchy of Namibian history, and it is easy to see why oral history collection has become such a hot political issue in a new African state striving to blend disparate tribal nations into a one nation "new Namibia".

The Namibian experience helps to illustrate the dangers of assuming that oral history can provide a "correct" or "agreed" version of events. It can only offer "perceived" versions. While these should be useful complements to the "received" version, and can go some way to helping peoples and nations draw strength from the rich diversity of their traditions, cultures and historical memories, they can also destabilise relations between groups. Oral history, like any "history", can both combat and fuel propaganda.

national priority and several Namibian cultural organisations have joined forces to set up a national archive and to disseminate oral materials as resources for educational, health, agricultural and cultural activities, using books and a new radio station called Katutura Community Radio [15].

A guide to using oral history in the school curriculum, published in Namibia and entitled *Speak for Yourself*, explores how important a knowledge of history can be to a growing sense of nationhood. By collecting oral history within their local community, pupils can uncover the "silences in Namibian history" and "present alternative versions of history": it may not be possible to prove which is correct, but they are "important in telling us what people believe [16]".

Oral artistry

In the same way that oral source material can be incorporated into the education system, so it can be adapted to communicate development messages, particularly in areas such as health and agriculture. Most development agencies now recognise that unless development messages make sense within the idiom of the target group they will not have an impact. This is a principle long held by the communications establishment, but one which has been too often ignored by development practitioners, not least because the need to consult, inform and convince people has been only fitfully acknowledged [17].

The theatre, song and storytelling of people's oral tradition is increasingly being used to convey health education messages. One such example is from Ban Vinai camp in northeast Thailand, where a health education programme was developed for the camp's 48,000 Hmong refugees (see p46). The project drew on traditional characters from Hmong folklore and dramatised them in a people's theatre which acted out health messages in the traditional Hmong oral genres of storytelling, proverbs, folksinging, rhyming chants and audience participation.

Using oral tradition and artistry as part of development communication is not simply a cunning form of propaganda and social marketing. It can also provide the idiom and opportunity for communities to talk back and express their views on development activities. The arts of theatre and storytelling have both a didactic and subversive function in all cultures. They provide ritual and artistic space in which it becomes relatively safe to say things which may not be acceptable if said directly and without "masks". In Mali, the

Rural theatre: an end or a means?

SOS Sahel's Drama Unit worked in a number of Bobo villages in the Tominian district of Mali. The project began in 1990 by adapting the traditional work songs which are sung by *griots* as accompaniment to seasonal agricultural labour. The *griots* were fully informed about the potential benefits of water-harvesting and reforestation and were trained to become "the holders of a basic technical knowledge, sought by their own community or even by neighbouring villages". The *griots* sang to people engaged in the new collective work which the project communities were doing on tree planting, soil and water conservation. As Alex Mavro, director of the Unit, explained, their improvised songs "soon expanded to include both technical encouragement and talk of a greener future [32]". More people were likely to hear these songs than to attend formal project meetings which might discuss the same issues.

In the evenings, over the next two years, the Drama Unit encouraged young villagers to act out the issues which concerned them about the development projects. The plays gradually became "more accomplished and increasingly frank", but the process was slow. Early productions seemed eager not to offend the outsiders and their efforts, but a new boldness emerged over time. The plays enacted tales of mistrust between villagers, of corrupt government forestry officials, and of fickle development workers who arrive with great promises and then lose interest in the project and move on to another village. There were also certain "pressure plays" which made direct requests for resources outside SOS Sahel's remit, such as grain banks, mills, health facilities and cash.

It was hoped that the plays would stimulate discussion and dialogue between the project and the villagers, and become a vital part of participatory monitoring and evaluation. This proved over-optimistic, as an evaluation in 1993 pointed out, not least because the critical issue of whether theatre was an end or a means remained unresolved [33]. The evaluators felt that the Drama Unit was working towards "rural theatre for development" as well as "the development of rural theatre"—both aims were valid but require different approaches and activities. In the end, the Unit's work achieved greater success in the latter role; local interest in community-authored drama and debate was enthusiastically revived. But the impact on the project work was minimal, for the Unit made little progress in achieving its development objectives. The evaluation concluded that it was a worthwhile experiment, but that the approach needs refining if it is to contribute as much to the art of development as it did to the art of performance.

drama unit of SOS Sahel used the traditional *griot* work song to convey agricultural and environmental information, but they also helped to develop a form of local theatre to discuss these development messages [18]. SOS Sahel discovered that this was an opportunity which the communities were glad to seize, but the project experienced difficulty in moving beyond providing entertainment, albeit of a thought-provoking kind, and

Culture and health education

Ban Vinai refugee camp, in an isolated hilly region of Thailand, contains some 48,000 Hmong crowded onto about 400 acres. Not only is this the biggest settlement in the region, surpassing even the provincial capital, but it is the largest gathering of Hmong in the world. Formerly living in scattered mountaintop villages in northern Laos, the people began their refugee existence when US forces withdrew in 1975 and a government hostile to the Hmong assumed power.

Appalling overcrowding and inadequate housing, sanitation and waste facilities caused severe health and hygiene problems in the camp. The conventional health education approach, with its implicit message that the Hmong were dirty and irresponsible about hygiene, was at best ineffective and at worst offensive. But when a new approach, building on Hmong folklore and traditional forms of communication, was tried, it proved to be far more successful. It incorporated two elements relevant to wider development programmes: a sensitivity to the history and culture of the people concerned, and a recognition of the specific problems and constraints of the surrounding environment.

A group of refugees, including traditional healers and Hmong elders, worked with a local Thai employee of the International Rescue Committee and Dwight Conquergood, an American performance ethnographer, to produce, by trial and error, an environmental health campaign using performance. In doing so, they built on the one thing in the camps which was as flourishing as the diseases spread by the poor sanitation: "No matter where you go in the camp, at almost any hour of the day or night, you can simultaneously hear two or three performances, from simple storytelling and folksinging to the elaborate collective ritual performances for the dead," wrote Conquergood [34].

The process of researching and developing the programme was as important as the end product. The team drew on stock characters and storylines in Hmong folklore and conveyed their messages using traditional forms of communication and education, such as proverbs and songs. Trial performances were staged to elicit audience feedback. Among the useful criticisms which helped the team develop and refine the programme was an elder's observation that the rhyming chants were not quite in keeping with traditional Hmong versification. He taught the young performers the correct patterns of speech, and ensured that the background music was authentic Hmong, rather than a version influenced by Thai or Western melodies.

On the health side, a key aspect was to develop understanding of the way in which the Hmong had formerly dealt with rubbish and sanitation, using methods which had been entirely appropriate to their environment. Instead of blaming the Hmong and trying to get them to change their behaviour on the basis that they caused the health problems, the important thing was to start with their radically changed living conditions and raise awareness of the implications of this for health. Thus the problem was located in the changed environmental circumstances; the solution was in adapting their practices.

The programme was effective, and Mother Clean, the collective creation of the performance company, had soon been integrated into camp culture and even featured in the important and elaborate Hmong New Year celebrations. However, with hindsight,

Conquergood realised that the so-called cross-cultural communication was still too one-way. The expatriate health professionals needed consciousness-raising, too; many were highly trained physicians and nurses but had little understanding of Hmong culture. They knew virtually nothing about the folk healers in the community, particularly the shamans, and were predisposed against them, seeing shamanism as "devil worship" and barbarism. As Conquergood puts it: "They desperately needed not just 'information' about Hmong culture, but serious interventions that would develop intercultural sensitivity and respect for difference." More opportunities for the Hmong to direct performances at the "experts", to educate them about their culture and life in the camp, would have reduced the lingering sense that it was only the Hmong who had something to learn, rather than something to teach others.

becoming a genuinely powerful tool for raising critical awareness and stimulating dialogue on development.

Listening to other forms of oral artistry and tradition can also provide important information for relief and development workers, and contribute to their understanding of people's way of life. As with the Dinka in southern Sudan (see p32), songs and stories can boost morale and reinforce social cohesion in times of crisis or change, but they can also convey new models for social behaviour. The messages they contain may be oblique, but are no less telling for that. Palestinian oral artistry, for example, has played a crucial part in the *intifada* or uprising which began in the Occupied Territories of the West Bank and Gaza Strip in 1987. A collection of some 250 stories provides graphic images of the changes in Palestinian society, the kind of social change which it is so vital to understand if development initiatives are to be targeted appropriately [19]. The stories reveal, for example, the much more active role that women in particular, but also children and young men, are taking in Palestinian society today. Development programmes in health, education and income generation need to take these changed roles into account in order to be effective.

Sharif Kanaana, who collected the stories, believes they set the agenda of the *intifada* by "explaining, rationalising, confirming, denying, ridiculing or supporting" various actions by Palestinian heroes and their Israeli occupiers. Women, particularly in their role as mothers, emerge from the legends as the mainstay of Palestinian society in crisis, its most supportive and indispensable group. Much is also revealed about the new active role of the children and young men in the territories, and the strong "son-mother team" which is seen as the foundation of the *intifada* and the new Palestinian social order. One of the stories is a particularly striking illustration of how this son-mother relationship and the mobilisation of children has come to be seen as so important a part of the Palestinian resistance to Israeli occupation:

> One time when the town [Gaza] was under curfew, a pregnant woman started having labour pains. The soldiers took her to a military hospital to give birth there. It turned out that she was pregnant with twin boys. The head of one of the babies came out first, he looked around and saw all these [Israeli] military uniforms, turned back to his brother and shouted, "Ahmed! Ahmed! We are surrounded, get some rocks!"

This story, while humorous at one level, is also extremely disturbing and socially revealing. It shows in no uncertain terms how both women and children are now expected to play a full and active part in Palestinian resistance, and how the whole of Palestinian society has assumed a confrontational role in the bitter struggle against Israeli occupation. The implications for women and children are obviously immense as the definition of what is "heroic" for them has changed enormously, and new demands have been placed on them.

Popular stories like these, composed in extreme conditions but often laced with humour, can throw a particularly sharp spotlight on societies undergoing rapid change. Legends, anecdotes and even jokes are often one of the first forms through which a society will express itself and acknowledge new experiences. Old stories and anecdotes are often reworked to reflect current concerns and preoccupations. Collection and interpretation of oral artistry can provide useful insights into the changing socio-economic circumstances of a community and could form a central part of pre-project research, complementing more conventional baseline surveys and needs assessments routinely carried out by development agencies.

Human rights

Human rights work is no longer considered simply as a branch of international law, but increasingly as a fundamental part of the development process. Development is about meeting human rights. Discussions about land rights, labour rights, trading rights, women's rights, children's rights, the rights of the disabled, and the rights to free association lie ever more at the heart of the development debate. In addition, as political, economic and ethnic tensions continue to flare into violence throughout the world, development workers are increasingly finding that the long-term impacts of conflict and human rights abuse—psychological, social, economic and cultural, as well as material and environmental—have increasingly to be considered in their work [20].

In the past, human rights work has often been dry and legalistic, but an increasing amount of monitoring and reporting now includes people's own words and accounts. A mix of oral testimony and legal analysis has become a standard part of the methodology [21]. Not only does this approach give more accuracy and impact, but by giving people a voice it returns an important element of power to the victims, beginning a process of confronting the violators and redressing the balance.

Oral testimony work in this field has two particular characteristics. First, in much human rights work the purpose is to collect evidence which will stand up in a court of law, so the testimony often needs to serve a legal as well as an analytical and historical function. Second, it usually involves the recounting of personal suffering and tragedy, and can be extremely painful for the teller—and for the listener.

All interviewing requires skill and sensitivity and can be therapeutic as well as informative, but human rights workers need additional training. Taking victims' testimonies can have a psychological as well as legal objective and it is essential to ensure that there is adequate support for the people recounting their experiences, and for those who have listened.

Land rights
Oral history is often an effective way to gather evidence for controversies over issues such as land rights, particularly when there is a clash between a "modern" western system and a traditional, probably unwritten, code of rights, in which the very concepts of "land" and "ownership" differ. On the island of Malai'ta in the Solomon Islands, oral history was used to

Being sure of the old before adapting to the new

The introduction to *Falafala ana Ano'i Kwara'ae* (The Tradition of Land in Kwara'ae) states:

> *The life of the Kwara'ae people is changing very fast. Many people in Kwara'ae are forgetting their old traditions or they are changing their old traditions to suit life in the present day and in future times to come. But if we want to change traditions of the past, we must first understand them before we choose what tradition is good for us to hold on to and what tradition is appropriate that we change. We must first be sure of the old traditions, before we choose what is suitable for life at this time or in times to come.*

This then is one of the purposes of collecting oral testimony: to document past tradition and provide a firm basis on which to deal with present and future concerns. This was a key reason why the Kwara'ae people of Mala'ita in the Solomon Islands supported the production of a dual-language booklet on traditional land rights and resource management. "Writing down custom was an exercise in salvaging traditional knowledge before it is lost with the death of older generations, and creating a written record of an oral tradition in a form that everyone can accept and abide by," adds anthropologist Ben Burt, who produced the book with Kwara'ae Michael Kwa'ioloa [35]. The text was discussed, corrected and approved by a wide range of people from the Kwara'ae community, as well as provincial leaders and representatives.

The "land book" project raised a number of important questions, not only, says Burt, "about the contradictions between 'tradition' and 'development' but about how we should document traditional culture [36]". For example, looking at land merely as an area of ground misses the essential point that land was valued for the natural resources of the forest ecosystem as a whole.

Land tenure was a system for allocating and managing these resources according to the values governing relationships in Kwara'ae society, and these were very different from the values served by Western notions of property rights and ownership. Thus, while land rights in the Solomons still determine who should control land and natural

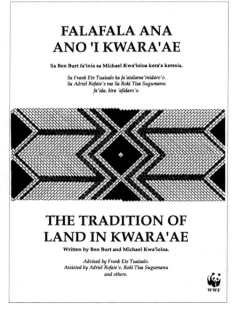

**FALAFALA ANA
ANO 'I KWARA'AE**

Sa Ben Burt fa'inia sa Michael Kwa'ioloa kera'a keresia.

Sa Frank Ete Tuaisalo ka fa'atalama'inidaro'o.
Sa Adriel Rofate'e ma Sa Roki Tisa Sugumanu
fa'ida, kira 'afidaro'o.

**THE TRADITION OF
LAND IN KWARA'AE**

Written by Ben Burt and Michael Kwa'ioloa.

*Advised by Frank Ete Tuaisalo.
Assisted by Adriel Rofate'e, Roki Tisa Sugumanu
and others.*

WWF

resources, in the context of the traditional economic and political system, they also act as a means of ensuring everyone has access to the resources they need to support themselves. In fact, they are "not so much a way of dividing land among people as a way of distributing people over land [37]."

Land rights are based not just on rules of inheritance but also on the values of sharing and helping, which the Kwara'ae call in English "love". Thus merely to document the rules without giving due importance to the underlying value system, which made it flexible enough to take account of circumstances and relationships, would have done scant justice to the tradition. Of course, these sorts of values do not fit easily into the kind of economic development now occurring in the Solomon Islands; hence the need to make changes either to the land rights or to the kind of development currently being embraced, the outcome of which is growing competition for land, the use of far larger areas than in the past, and a temptation to go for short-term gains, now that people are no longer dependent solely on the natural resources of the forest for their livelihood.

While in one sense there was a desire for a book of "law" that codified traditional norms and values, and would help to resolve disagreements about land rights and settle disputes, it seems, as the introduction suggests, that the first stage was to establish an agreed understanding and record of the past before it could be adapted for the future. This understanding was especially important for the younger generation, who had lost touch with tradition, and the governing elite, many of whom share an education and outlook which reflect Western rather than Kwara'ae concepts.

investigate and communicate the traditional land ownership systems of the Kwara'ae people, in the face of competing claims on land suddenly valuable for cash cropping or development. Government attempts to interpret local land tenure systems in terms of western categories of ownership had proved simplistic and inequitable and the issue was threatening to divide Kwara'ae society. The World Wide Fund for Nature (WWF) supported efforts to consult community elders about the nature and history of land tenure and with them to produce a bilingual booklet. This document was offered to the government as a guide for determining more appropriate legal decisions over land disputes.

In Canada, legal arguments over traditional land rights have become especially extensive in the past 20 years and oral testimony is accepted as vital to such cases. Hugh Brody, a researcher at Britain's Scott Polar Institute, describes one land-use documentation project in his book *Maps and Dreams* (see overleaf).

Maps and dreams

In the five centuries of white European colonisation of North America the earlier settlers of the continent, the Indians, have been used when convenient and brushed aside when not; and in tune with this, mythologised as formidably warlike, but economically insignificant. The British recognised all the lands west of the Allegheny Mountains as Indian in 1763— when they wanted the Indians as allies—and in Canada today the rights of Indians to land are governed by a series of subsequent treaties. In 1899, Treaty 8 opened up northeast British Columbia to white settlement, the Indians ceding their rights in return for a trivial annuity and an education service, but retaining, in addition to small residential reserves, hunting rights over the whole area wherever it was not settled. And in this harsh frontier region, ranging from the Rocky Mountain foothills and forests to prairie and sub-arctic wilderness, white settlers and the Indians still co-exist—in largely separate cultural and economic worlds.

Throughout most of the continent the Indians, attacked, driven off their lands, demoralised by disease and cultural denial, had been all but exterminated. But in the 1970s, from their remaining bases, above all in the far north, a new Indian politics of "Red power" emerged, demanding equal citizenship, control over their resources and recognition of their socio-economic systems, and denouncing many of the legal interpretations of the treaties as fraudulent. In Canada this growing political confidence has continued into the 1990s. Today more than a third of the country is in the grip of some form of native legal or political action. Indians right across Canada have become aware that they can win court actions and that their own oral memories have proved crucial in this. Their demands, as polar researcher Hugh Brody predicted, "will not go away: a final genocide is not going to be achieved [38]".

On the British Columbia frontier, the focus of Indian fear and resistance was the impact of the construction of a natural gas pipeline through the area of the reserves, close to the Alaskan Highway. In 1977 the Union of British Columbia Indian Chiefs called for a public enquiry into the socio-economic effects and the Canadian government decided to fund a preparatory land-use enquiry. It was this which brought Brody, who had previously studied the Inuit farther north in the Northwest Territories and in Labrador, to live for 18 months on the British Columbia reserves in 1978-9. His book, *Maps and Dreams*, is part of the enquiry's findings [39].

Brody came to the Doig River Reserve to work on a survey, using a combination of sources but above all oral evidence from the Indians themselves, with the purpose of describing their economic life and land use in the closest possible detail. In the context of the Canadian north such surveys have proved a crucial instrument for challenging "fatalism" over the Indians' economic and social future. White politicians and administrators have continually insisted that their only hope was through some form of "development" rather than their own culture or economy. But these were mere assumptions, for little was known or understood about the Indians' use of land. Stereotypes about hunters and primitive economies, frontiersmen's self-serving prejudices and the Indians' own inclination to remain hidden, all contributed to drastic misunderstandings of Indian economic interests.

"Few facts ever disturbed the white man's myths, and no account of Indian economic needs ever challenged his purpose," wrote Brody [40].

Beginning in 1973 in the Northwest Territories, and since conducted in Labrador, the Yukon, northern Quebec and northern Ontario, these surveys vary somewhat in character, but always the key method is the mapping, by individual Indian hunters, trappers, fishers, and berry pickers, of all the land they ever used in their lifetimes, encircling on the maps their hunting areas species by species, and marking gathering locations and camping sites. The results not only confirmed and amplified what was known about the past, but also "showed something almost no one, including many of the scientists involved, expected: the people's systems extended into the present [41]". The Indian economy was shown as still a viable basis for cultural and material well-being—well worth defending.

In *Maps and Dreams,* Brody illustrates a series of maps, showing how they are combined in analysis to plot the land-use patterns of each community. He discusses some of the problems he encountered: for example, it was not possible to persuade older Indians to draw different maps for different time periods. He argues that despite their unfamiliarity with maps and mapping, the results can be shown to be highly reliable because of the many "striking correspondences" between those of different mappers. Each hunter did his own map, often without having seen anyone else's, yet "there are lines that again and again appear in the same places. There are whole circles that neatly sit one on top of the other [42]". Equally strikingly, the maps made in different communities fit logically together.

"Research done as part of a political process can actually be conducive to the most reliable results," Brody suggests [43]. And the facts revealed have been equally important politically:

> The Indians have supposedly been on the verge of disappearing since soon after they were first encountered by Europeans; hunters have been thought to have no economic life since they first aroused European sympathy, or dismay...The result of a land-use and occupancy study is a crucial first step away from uninformed and stereotypic pessimism [44].

The right to self-definition

Few societies or communities are so equitable that everyone has the same social and economic status. Certain individuals and groups find themselves on the margins of society because of gender, age, disability, ethnicity, religion or caste. Giving these groups their own voice through the collection and communication of their personal testimony is an important way of making them more "visible" and enabling their version of reality, not an outsider's view, to be heard.

The collection and dissemination of oral testimony—in books, at conferences and through the media and performance arts—has become a particularly important part of disabled people's campaigns to articulate their experience and challenge the way society perceives and treats them. It has provided a starting point for a growing movement to realise the rights of disabled people. In a recent book entitled *Disability, Liberation and Development*, Peter Coleridge of the British NGO Oxfam, collected interviews with 300 disabled people in Africa, Asia and the Middle East [22]. More than most, disabled people have been the victims of other people's language, which often stigmatises, undermines, discounts and isolates them. As Coleridge points out: "Words like 'poor', 'victim', 'suffering', 'afflicted', 'confined' and 'restricted' all reinforce the notion of disabled people as sick and helpless."

Because of labels like these, the opportunity for disabled people to speak up and describe themselves becomes all the more important. It gives them the chance to define their own world for a change and to challenge the language which others use to describe them and the attitudes which it reveals. Nawaf Kabbara from Lebanon illustrates the first stage in such a process, that of making oneself heard:

> When you are managing a life outside society, you have to make society aware that you are there. Only then can you be integrated into society. We have hardly started at the beginning of this process. I mean you can't be integrated if you are not even recognised as being there! This is what people do not understand. I have been challenged on this many times in Lebanon....But this is the way for people to see that we are there. That we exist.

Joshua Malinga in Zimbabwe feels the same about the need for disabled people to mobilise themselves and to be heard:

> If you see yourself as a minority and as a group that is not taking part in society, you have to find a solution, and one of the solutions is that you organise as a group to create a voice, and then you get listened to by the powers-that-be.

Malinga goes on to explain how this mobilisation also means confronting the rehabilitation professionals.

> The point is that they believe they have solutions to our problems. They do not see us as belonging to society, they think we belong to them, they have to keep files on us throughout our lives, and decide when we should see the doctor and so on. But I

want to decide when I see the doctor! They have enjoyed power
and control over us for a long period. We have to understand
that we are talking about an attitude here. Changing attitudes is
a very difficult thing.

One of the strongest sentiments which emerges from many of
the testimonies in Coleridge's book is the passionate desire of
disabled people to be recognised as whole in their own right,
and not to be constantly seen as incomplete. The words of
disabled people, like the words of many who have been spoken
for, tend to challenge stereotypes. Oral testimony can be a
particularly powerful way for people to assert their own reality,
to show up how partial the views of outsiders are, to describe
how their rights have been ignored or abused, and then to
express their ideas about how they would like to see these
rights fulfilled.

Development education

Oral testimony can also be applied to the development process
as part of advocacy or information programmes. An increasing
number of NGOs, in both the North and South, are launching
advocacy campaigns to bring the issues of underdevelopment
and inequality to the attention of policy makers and publics
throughout the world.

Experience has shown that one of the most successful ways
to make an impact is to personalise specific issues. This has to
be done with sensitivity and honesty, however. Much NGO
advocacy work still draws on rather opportunistic or superficial
life story work, which might have more impact if it were more
rigorous. A similarly token approach often characterises NGO
marketing and fundraising strategies, in which campaigns have
been built around negative images of a disaster-ridden Third
World, presenting people as powerless and trapped, with little
or no hint of their culture, achievements, innovations or the rich
variety of experience they have to offer. Awareness is growing,
however, and some agencies issue guidelines to encourage a
more thorough approach and a more honest and rounded
picture. When the whole story of people's lives is allowed to
come through in their own words, it has more impact than any
number of attempts to speak for them.

The same principles apply to the use of oral history material in development education material for schools. One good example is the Minority Rights Group's bilingual *Voices* series, designed for schools in Britain. *Voices from Somalia*, for example, contains the life stories of several young Somalis who recently fled their country and are living as refugees in Britain [23]. They describe their early lives in Somalia, their experience of war, their flight from home and their very different life as refugees. The one-dimensional view of the refugee as dependent and helpless thus gives way to a more rounded picture featuring resilience and resourcefulness, and also offers a valuable perspective on the British community in which they find themselves.

Development methodologies

Oral history techniques are being increasingly accepted as a valuable addition to the range of methodologies that make up Participatory Rural Appraisal (PRA). In the past decade there has been a belated acknowledgement that "the poor" are not a homogenous group, that they are capable and knowledgeable, and that development workers should learn both from them and with them. PRA is the successor to Rapid Rural Appraisal, and is supposed to be less "quick and dirty", less extractive and more consultative. PRA recognises the limitations of traditional scientific survey techniques, which seldom involve people in creative discussion of their own development priorities. At the heart of the new PRA methodologies, therefore, lies a concern for ensuring participation, and for using methods which not only operate within the idiom of the people being consulted, but enable them to experiment and employ their own terminology.

The "menu" of PRA methods is extensive, drawing on applied anthropology, farming and ecosystems research, and participatory extension methods. Development workers, researchers and the communities with which they work, select a variety of methods from the menu including individual and group interviews; mapping; transects, modelling and diagramming; and ranking and scoring exercises. PRA practitioners have come to regard oral history as an integral part of their approach and it is a central feature of methods such as historical mapping and modelling; trend analysis; and time-lines and chronologies.

PRA is proving particularly useful at the project identification stage, when research is undertaken and appraisal made of the existing situation and of priorities for the future, as well as at the evaluation stage. The collection of individual life stories or community histories can prove a powerful entry point into discussion and understanding of current conditions.

The mixing of visual and oral historical information is a particularly exciting innovation to have emerged from the use of oral history within PRA. Robert Chambers, for example, has described how visual techniques, such as diagramming and mapping, can combine with oral testimony to illustrate "the shape of the past" [24]. Indeed, most PRA activities involving oral history collection have combined it with visual diagramming and mapping. The PRA experience has shown that people's ability to express themselves verbally can be heightened if they can simultaneously present things visually— particularly where the process of being interviewed is an unusual one, and one which may be acting as a brake on their oral fluency. Diagrams can be drawn on paper or made on the ground, using pebbles and counters. People can take researchers on a tour of a transect (sample route) of an area and talk them through its history, physically showing them how and where things used to be done. The next chapter explains these visual techniques and gives examples of their application.

PRA, as it is currently practised, is fundamentally a small group activity, not necessarily well suited to exploring the more private realms of people's lives. This kind of testimony needs to be collected in a more secluded setting and requires more time (see Chapter Four).

Monitoring and evaluation

While much of the early part of project work involves looking back at the past as a means of analysing patterns of poverty, at a certain point the project itself requires retrospective analysis. Many development agencies produce written documents as part of the evaluation process, but the inclusion of oral accounts can introduce a wider dimension and correct an almost inevitable bias towards quantitative goals and objectives. By comparing conditions before and after development interventions, in terms of people's subjective historical experience and not simply in terms of the project's data and reports, oral testimony can play a valuable part in any evaluation or review—and should include the experience of project workers and "beneficiaries". As such, oral testimony can play a valuable role in participatory evaluation, which is a continuing process rather than an "event". The case study of Save the Children Fund's review of Somalia's national immunisation programme, and the research projects stimulated by the Sahel Oral History Project, both described in Chapter Five, provide some examples of this testimony-based approach to evaluation and monitoring.

For large-scale and long-term projects of the kind favoured and funded by the World Bank and other major donors, a historical testimony-based approach to evaluation may be particularly valuable. The life span of this type of project can be decades. Interventions are often on a scale which means that the way of life of many inhabitants of the project area can be changed in more ways than the original project designers intended—or acknowledged. The wider impact of such projects is seldom picked up, or even sought, by normal indicators, but might emerge more clearly through an oral history of the project provided by staff and the target population, as well as by other affected communities. People who are displaced or resettled as a consequence of dam-building and other large-scale development projects are often inadequately and inappropriately compensated and suffer in ways which are rarely documented. Investigating cultural and personal damage and disruption is seldom part of the terms of reference, so that those who benefit from such schemes continue to promote them, and the real costs remain hidden [25].

One example of using oral testimony in evaluation is a 1983 study, carried out by the UN's International Labour Office (ILO), of a project in India started 30 years earlier [26].

The project, begun in 1953 and funded by the Norwegian government, modernised fishing technology in three coastal villages in the state of Kerala. Motor boats, fish-processing technology, ice-making and freezing were introduced into these communities with the aim of increasing productivity and boosting exports through improved fish preservation. Additional health services and sanitation initiatives were also developed. ILO undertook the study three decades later to assess the project's impact on women in the area.

Women had not been targeted by the project which, "as it was conceived and designed, was mainly geared towards men in the community. Since women did not go out fishing, it was assumed that change in the technology of fishing was of no direct concern to them." In fact, as the women had always processed and marketed the fish, this proved to be a false assumption even in economic terms. Over the next 30 years the modernisation of the fishing industry in the area did have a major impact on women's lives, reshaping their work and social status, as well as affecting their health, education and family planning.

The ILO study employed conventional socio-economic surveys, but combined these with intensive life story interviews, the "autobiographical method" as the study document describes it. A sample of 30 women in the area was selected and case studies taken of their families, using life stories of the women themselves but including information gleaned from them on the lives of their family members from current and preceding generations spanning the 30-year period. This allowed the researchers to cast a wider net: "On average it was possible to collect information for each family based on 26 related couples covering three generations. Thus information was collected on 784 couples in all."

The ripple effect of this kind of interviewing meant it was time-consuming, but comprehensive. The result was a very full picture of the changes in women's lives throughout the 30 years. The study found that new work opportunities had opened up for women in trading, processing of fish products and net-making. These activities were all generally better-paying than those available to women prior to mechanisation and some women had become independent entrepreneurs. Women's health also improved during the period as a result of better services, higher incomes and increased educational opportunities. The study's socio-economic surveys, which indicated some of these changes, were brought to life by the actual experiences of the women interviewed.

This example shows how oral testimony can play a central part in project histories and evaluation. In this case, the study revealed changes which were not anticipated, some of which were beneficial, although they could have been more positive if the technological innovation had not been concentrated exclusively on the men's activities. Not all projects have such positive side effects. Those projects which are hailed as successful because they have met their chosen targets, may well have had negative side effects in areas which remain unacknowledged, unrecorded, and even undetected—because it is usually the poorest who have most to lose from mega-projects and the least chance to voice or document their objections or experiences. A broader "unofficial history" which draws on their testimony can set the record straight.

CHAPTER FOUR

WAYS OF LISTENING
The art of collecting testimony

Oral testimony may be sought and used in a variety of contexts, as a project in itself or as one of a number of methods in a wider research or appraisal activity. Whatever the context, it is vital to spend time at the beginning clarifying the aims and objectives of the exercise, and examining the best ways to achieve them.

Planning a project

During the planning stage, the themes for investigation should be developed and discussed with the participants in the project and with the community concerned. A fundamental part of this stage has to be a consideration not just of the social, economic, environmental or working worlds of the potential interviewees, but also of the cultural context in which the interviewing will take place. Appropriate decisions can then be made about which interviewing methods to use.

Cross-cultural dimensions

While the interview is now a common form of enquiry and communication in the West—where a job interview is a prerequisite for most employment, the media feature endless interviews, both informative and entertaining, and few people escape having to take part in polls and questionnaires—this is by no means a universal experience. As British anthropologist Charles Briggs has observed, in some societies the interview is not an established type of speech event, and there can often be an incompatibility between standard interview techniques and indigenous systems of communication [1]. This incompatibility can create problems for people who, as interviewees, are forced to express themselves in an unfamiliar speech format. In particular, the interview form has a tendency to put unnatural pressure on people to find ready answers, to be concise and to summarise a variety of complex experiences and intricate knowledge [2]. It may also mean that researchers and interviewers unwittingly violate local communication norms relating to turn-taking, the order of topics for discussion or various rituals attached to storytelling. In some societies, individual interviews are considered dangerously intimate encounters. In others, the recounting of group history can be a sacred ritual and certain people must be consulted before others. Sometimes a number of clearly prescribed topics should be used to start proceedings, while other topics may be taboo, or should not be introduced until a particular level of intimacy and trust has been achieved.

In many societies, community or clan history is the vested interest of particular people or a designated caste, such as the *griots* of West Africa. They will often adapt their account to a particular audience, tailoring it to focus on the ancestors of their listeners. Alongside the right to tell, there is often a reward: payment in cash or kind for the teller. Storytelling may also have a seasonal dimension. In Ladakh, for example, winter is the time for telling stories. It is considered an inappropriate activity during the busy summer months when the agricultural workload is at its peak, as a local saying makes clear: "As long as the earth is green, no tale should be told [3]." It would be an ill-prepared and disappointed oral testimony project that set out to collect traditional stories in Ladakh during the summer!

There may also be special rituals of rendition which require certain elders to act as witnesses and checks on the history or stories being recounted. The proper setting for the recounting of a community history may be a feast with a minimum number present. Such conditions affect the collection of oral history and can sometimes even make it impossible, as Lomo Zachary, a Sudanese researcher, found when he tried to gather information about the origins and relations of various Ugandan clans living as refugees in South Sudan:

> *I approached several clan historians but all were asking me for a "Calabash"—meaning some liquor...After requesting some liquor most told me that they were unable to narrate me any stories because there were no esteemed witnesses or observers.*

Usually when such clan histories are told to clansmen or a group of interested young clansmen there is someone also well versed in the clan history who makes corrections when necessary. Sometimes they have long debates on a controversial item in the history. For example, the storyteller might skip or include a false family line of a particular clansman. Here the observer or witness has to interpose immediately with concrete proofs....So all gave me a similar response: "My son, I am indeed grateful for your wise request for knowing where we originated from, how we have come to be separated and how we handle our affairs. I could have given you an elaborate history of our people but as you know, we are all scattered at this time. We have lost all our animals. There are no more tribal palavers where our people could be gathered....It could be during such sittings that our wise children could now put down all our cultures and traditions. Please accept my sincere apologies [4]."

It is critically important to be aware of these different conceptual and cultural dimensions to interviewing and to historical information. A vital part of any preparation for an oral testimony project should involve learning about the norms of what Briggs describes as people's "communicative repertoire": its particular forms, its special events, its speech categories and its taboos [5]. The most fundamental rule is to be sensitive to customary modes of speech and communication and allow people to speak on their own terms.

Methods of collection

There are a number of different kinds of interview. The most wide-ranging form is the individual life story. This allows a person to narrate the story of his or her whole life in all its dimensions: personal, spiritual, social and economic. Another kind is the single-issue interview which seeks to gain testimony about a particular aspect or period of a person's life. As Chapter Three showed, the object might be to hear about someone's working life, perhaps with an emphasis on indigenous knowledge, or to listen to their experiences during an event or episode such as a famine or a time of conflict or displacement. In addition to individual interviews, oral testimony can also be collected in focus group discussions, community interviews or by diary interviewing. When choosing the method(s) to be

Topics for a life story

One of the great advantages of a life story interview is that it tracks a person's experience across all the different economic and social sectors of their life. To do this effectively, an interview needs to cover a certain cross-section of topics.

Some basic biographical data should be covered at the start, such as: the narrator's name; when and where they were born; their occupation(s); where their parents live(d); what their parents do/did; what family they have.

These and similar questions often provide a useful "warm-up" during which both parties can get the feel of each other and begin to develop a rapport. Once again, the communicative repertoire of various societies will differ and certain greetings and topics may have to be followed in a prescribed order.

The other topics to be covered in a life story can be divided into three broad sections.

Issues of family and early life

- Family background: grandparents, elderly relations, extended family, and their influence.
- Parents: where they came from, their occupations and roles in the family, their personalities, the narrator's relationship with them.
- Brothers, sisters and childhood friends: children's responsibilities, games and leisure activities, childhood journeys; what happened to siblings and friends in later life.
- Everyday life: the household environment; who did the domestic work, cooking etc; food and meal times etc.
- Special occasions: weddings, funerals, festivals and initiations.
- Local geography: the community, village or town; communal areas, land rights and ownership; markets, meeting places and other significant places; neighbours, important people and interesting characters.
- Social and cultural life: religion and politics; education and instruction at home, school or work; important friendships, influences and ambitions.

---

employed, it is important to bear in mind the objectives of the project and the kind of testimony required.

Life story interviews

These are normally private, one-to-one encounters between interviewer and narrator. Sessions should be held at a time convenient to the interviewee and in a suitable location, preferably somewhere which offers seclusion, comfort and familiarity. There is often no better place than the narrator's home.

In some societies, a one-to-one interview may not be acceptable, particularly for women, and one or more observers

Working life

- Occupation(s) inside and outside the home: domestic, agricultural, vocational, professional, formal, informal, paid and unpaid.
- How the skills were learnt; the work environment; what the work involves and who with; any formal or informal training or apprenticeship.
- Any changes of occupation and why; successes and failures in working life.
- Other income-generating opportunities, eg crafts, brewing, trading.
- A typical working day: seasonal variations.
- Important influences at work: mentors, colleagues, friends, enemies.
- Work-related organisations: cooperatives, informal groups, professional organisations, unions; any social life connected with work.
- Wider changes affecting work: environmental, industrial, political etc.

Adult family and social life

- Central relationships: single, married, separated, divorced or widowed; monogamous or polygamous; the meeting of partner(s), their background and occupation; any wedding; setting up or joining a household, who controls money and assets, the division of work and decision-making; expectations and ideals of marriage, the family home, children, childbirth, family planning, child care, ideals of parenting, affection and discipline; hopes and ambitions for children; the deaths of partners and family members. If single or childless: by choice or circumstance; attitude of others to this.
- Leisure activities: hobbies; friends and relationships; music, dance, drama, storytelling; religious or cultural festivals and entertainments; local groups or clubs; the community, the neighbours.
- Old age: becoming grandparents and/or other rights, responsibilities, privileges or difficulties which come with age.

will need to be present. This can serve the additional function of testing and cross-checking information as observers interrupt to challenge or correct the interviewee. However, it can also mean that information is distorted. In some situations, observers can act as censors and indeed may be there specifically to intimidate: husbands observing wives; parents observing children; or officials observing a community living in fear or repression [6]. While it is important to conform to the communicative repertoire of the people being interviewed, it pays to be aware that there may be more dubious aspects to observation and extra participation. Gender can also be an inhibiting factor and as a general rule interviewer and narrator should be the same sex (for a fuller discussion of this, see Chapter Six) [7].

An average life story interview may need two or three sessions and can take anything from one to eight hours. Breaking up the interview into separate sessions gives people time to remember and explore the past and makes recollection more of a process than an occasion. It takes the pressure off a single session, when the narrator might feel obliged to cram everything in. Things triggered in one session can be reflected upon by the narrator in peace and then brought to the next. The interviewer can similarly benefit from the pause between sessions.

It is important to remember that a life story interview can often have a profound effect on the interviewee, who may never have told anyone their memories before and certainly is unlikely to have recalled their whole life in the course of a few hours. For most people, recounting their life story is a positive, if emotional, experience from which they can gain much satisfaction and a renewed sense of perspective, but the listener should always ensure that the narrator is comfortable at the end of the interview and is surrounded by the support they need, whether from family or friends.

Family-tree interviewing
In the course of a life story interview, the narrator will describe many members of his or her family from contemporary or previous generations. These people will obviously be mentioned largely in terms of their impact on the narrator. However, as has been seen in the ILO fisherwomen study (see p58), it is possible to focus on these other family members in more depth by asking the narrator to supply second-hand accounts of their relatives' lives. This technique is perhaps best described as family-tree interviewing.

The ILO study was particularly concerned with changes in the women's lives over the past 30 years and so each woman in the sample was asked to give her version of the life stories of her mother, grandmothers, sisters, aunts, and female cousins. This process obviously takes up much more time, but it does give an interesting ripple effect to any study. It is perhaps most useful when one is looking for trends, rather than the specific detail of direct personal experience. An alternative, which is still more time-consuming but also a more direct measure of change, is to interview two generations from the same family.

Single-issue testimony

Single-issue interviews may be carried out on a one-to-one or group basis, and focus on a specific aspect of the narrator's life. As such they can be shorter than a life story, but more detailed. Single-issue interviews can yield valuable insights for many development and relief activities (see Chapter Three). They are the main method of learning about a particular event, such as drought, or for an investigation into a particular area of knowledge or experience. For example, they might involve interviewing farmers about land use and water conservation methods, or a traditional healer about botany and plant use. They require the interviewer to have more detailed background or technical knowledge of the subject matter than is necessary for a more wide-ranging life story.

Diary interviewing

Diary interviewing is a method which is increasingly being used by social scientists. It involves selecting a sample of people who contribute regular diary entries as part of a continuing and long-term study of social trends. Such a study might ask people to report on specific issues or it might seek more general life story material. The participants make a commitment to keep a written or oral, tape-recorded diary. Entries might be made on a daily, weekly, monthly or annual basis, and are then sent in and analysed centrally, over time.

Alternatively, diary interviewing can involve a less rigorous procedure whereby the participant is interviewed at key moments over a period of time. In a study of indigenous agricultural practices, for example, these might include particular times during the cropping calendar such as land preparation, sowing, weeding, harvesting and threshing. In a more general life story study, such moments might include religious festivals, rites of passage or different stages of educational or working life. The objective of diary interviewing is therefore to collect a running progress of a person's experience over time and not just retrospectively.

Group interviews

Oral testimony can also be collected through group work.

Indeed, in many societies, group interviews may be more in keeping with the customary ways of communicating. If the concept of a one-to-one interview seems unusual or unnatural, the format of group discussions or public meetings may be more familiar and oral testimony collection can be adapted accordingly.

Groups can bring out the best and the worst in people. Sometimes, by taking the focus off individuals, they make them less inhibited, but the opposite can occur just as easily. A group may subtly pressurise people towards a socially acceptable testimony or a mythical representation of the past or of a current issue which everyone feels is "safe" to share and which may be in some sense idealised. Communal histories gathered in this way can involve a powerful process of myth construction or fabulation which misrepresents the real complexity of the community. At worst, this can develop into a persistent false consciousness which can only tolerate the good things, and remembers "how united we all were", or which exaggerates the totality of suffering and recalls "how bad everything was [8]". The voices of the less confident, the poorer and the powerless, are less likely to be heard, and so the variety of experience and the clashes and conflicts within a community may well remain hidden.

But groups can also be especially productive, as members "spark" off one another. Memories are triggered, facts can be verified or checked, views can be challenged and the burning issues of the past can be discussed and argued about again in the light of the present. Group work can also increase rapport between project workers/interviewers and the community, encouraging people to come forward for one-to-one sessions if appropriate. Two kinds of group work are appropriate to oral testimony collection: small focus group discussions and larger community interviews.

Focus group discussions developed as an important part of market research, but are now used widely on an inter-disciplinary basis as a means of assessing attitudes and opinions. In this context, they are a particularly useful forum for discussing both the past and the major issues of the day. Focus groups are particularly appropriate for collecting testimony from people who may be very reserved on a one-to-one basis, but draw confidence from being in a familiar group.

Children are a good example of this.

The idea is to bring a group together—preferably between five and 12 people—to discuss a particular issue or a number of issues. They should be a homogenous group made up of participants of the same sex and largely equal in social status, knowledge and experience so that confidence is generally high and no-one feels threatened. The discussion should last for one to two hours, with the participants sitting comfortably and facing each other in a circle. Several consecutive sessions can be held if necessary.

Social scientist Krishna Kumar notes that the main emphasis in a focus group is the interaction between the participants themselves, and not that between participants and interviewer [9]. Focus groups are therefore guided by a "moderator" rather than an interviewer, whose role is to steer the discussion and ask some probing questions by adopting a posture of "sophisticated naïveté". This encourages the group to talk in depth with confidence, but also to be ready to spell things out for the outsider. The moderator's role also involves countering the two main constraints on a focus group: dominance of the proceedings by so-called "monopolisers"; and a sense of group pressure which can build up from a majority viewpoint and which then discourages a minority of participants from expressing their views.

Community interviews involve larger groups and may resemble public meetings more than group discussions. Their emphasis is different, too. The main interaction of a community interview is between the interviewer and the community. The ideal size is around 30 people, but no more, and two interviewers will be needed for such an event. Their role is a directly questioning one, but they must still take responsibility for balancing participation in the meeting with guiding the interview. Having two interviewers can be confusing and their respective roles should be well defined in advance of the interview, to ensure that they do not speak at the same time or interrupt each other's train of enquiry.

The advantage of a community interview is the opportunity it provides for gathering a wide cross-section of people together at one time. This is particularly useful at the outset of a project, for example, when background information is being collected or future interviewees are being sought and selected. It is also useful midway or at the end of the process of collecting interviews, when certain details or views need to be tested or checked. It can provide the occasion for a number of "straw polls" and hand counts in order to learn how many people share experiences or hold similar views. Finally, both group and community meetings are especially useful for the "return" of oral testimony and the findings of PRA exercises. They can act as a review mechanism and can encourage decision-making based on the testimonies collected.

Oral artistry

While the main method of collecting oral testimony is by recording interviews, it may be appropriate to include oral artistry, through which people can speak volumes about their past, their present and their hopes for the future. As has been noted, listening to and collecting songs, stories, legends, poems and drama can form an important part of oral testimony work as it relates to development ideas and practice.

P G N'Diaye, a consultant for UNESCO, describes oral tradition as "the oral transmission of ideas, customs and emotions which belong to a society [10]." In most cultures special artists are responsible for creating and maintaining oral tradition. Some forms of oral tradition, such as genealogies or climate calendars, have a specific record-keeping or technical function. Others are more essentially artistic, and help maintain the norms, conventions and organisation of a society.

One particularly important feature of oral works of art is that they rarely have a bound and final version like a book; more often they continue to be developed and adapted in performance. Traditional songs often accrue new meanings or come to refer to several similar events in history, and past events are usually given a present gloss, laced with contemporary references for today's audience. Thus, while it is difficult to speak of oral artistry as "objective" history, because of its organic nature, it nevertheless yields valuable information about social change, archetypal events and community responses past and present [11].

Oral artistry frequently has a didactic as well as a descriptive purpose. Stories, songs and histories contribute to the process of socialisation, providing a means of learning about a people's

Griots in Mali listen to the playback of their work songs, later adapted to convey environmental information (see Rural Theatre, p45).

codes and values, and of passing on good practice and the received wisdom of that society. Tales and proverbs about wise and foolish farmers, greedy merchants or careless parents, all represent advice which has been tried and tested in the past, or adapted or invented for a changing world. Development workers can often profit from listening to such tales, as they reveal much about a society's values, and can usefully be incorporated into the technical or educational components of development programmes.

But oral artistry is not only a medium for the establishment view. As well as conserving particular norms, it can become the means by which to challenge and subvert them. A new idea, or the rising consciousness of a marginalised group, can find its rallying point in a song or a story which attacks or ridicules the status quo. Because of its inherent elements of participation, performance and adaptability, oral artistry can be especially democratic. Much of it, except the most complex or sacred sagas, can be shared and passed on. Performances and renditions are often interactive and allow criticism and contribution from the audience. Little is cast in stone and the content is often vested with a high degree of public ownership, and open to scrutiny and discussion. This can have important benefits for development programmes, since ideas can be both expressed and challenged through these media.

When collecting songs or stories, however, it is vital to be aware of the particular conventions of each genre. This may demand a tone or posture that deliberately exaggerates a certain attitude or line of thought, which the inexperienced listener may take too literally, unaware of the intended irony, hyperbole or propaganda. When Megan Vaughan collected women's pounding songs in Malawi (see p28), she discovered them to be "an acceptable anti-male form which contain the possibility of expressing sexual antagonism in a socially acceptable way". In order to judge "how far [the songs] are simply part of a continuous concern over marital relations—the nature of the genre rather than the true reflection of events", Vaughan had to become very familiar with the women's use of the genre [12]. Only then could she give realistic interpretations of the songs she collected and identify in them the glimpses into factual experience which related to the particular phenomenon of marital breakdown caused by the famine, as distinct from the conventions of the genre. She was able to conclude: "The songs and testimonies, if treated with caution, are indispensable to any analysis of the famine."

Oral artistry can be researched formally, by recording the performances of professional artists, or informally by listening to and transcribing the songs, stories and theatre commonly used by ordinary people. As noted earlier, the formal performances of singers or storytellers may require the fulfilment of certain rites of rendition, and payment may be needed in some form. More everyday pieces, such as working songs or simple stories, can be recorded on the spot. Most short tales, myths or legends can be picked up as they are passed around by word of mouth. They can be recorded as a set piece or interviewers can encourage narrators to tell such tales during interviews. Whenever oral artistry is being recorded in performance, however, it is important that the technical process of recording should not intrude upon or change the event itself. A high level of trust is necessary between performers and those doing the recording to ensure that the event goes off naturally, and that performers and audience feel no threat to the privacy and integrity of the occasion.

Listening to children

Much of the above discussion has assumed that the narrator of oral testimony is an adult. There are, however, a growing number of occasions when oral testimony is collected from children.

More than most groups, children have been "spoken for", and often misunderstood or misrepresented. Identified as a priority group in many development programmes, children need to be directly consulted on matters that affect their education and welfare. The United Nations Convention on the Rights of the Child specifically includes their right to be consulted and to represent themselves [13]. Children in especially difficult circumstances, such as street children, need to voice their own views of the way they live and to relate their personal histories if development and social workers are going to understand their situation and provide appropriate support. The importance, for therapeutic reasons, of children being allowed to speak out and describe human rights abuses against them is likewise increasingly gaining recognition. The family tracing programmes described in Chapter Three are another example of work which requires testimony from children. Finally, children can play an important role as guardians—and innovators—of oral artistry by preserving, adapting and inventing stories, rhymes and songs.

If interviews are difficult for some adults, they can be especially hard for children. As one study on the subject points out: "It must be remembered that interviewing is an adult form of enquiry [14]." Interviews may be particularly stressful for children because of the formal nature of the occasion, the presence of strangers, and the pressure to perform and do the right thing. At a very basic level, young children may not have developed sufficient language and conceptual skills to handle an interview. As Naomi Richman has observed in her manual for development and relief workers, *Communicating with Children*, these pressures can often combine so that it becomes easy for an interviewer to make children say what he or she wants them to say, however unwittingly. Alternatively, children may clam up completely and be unable to speak because of anxiety about the occasion or the subject matter [15].

Collecting children's oral testimony therefore requires particular sensitivity and training, but there are also some basic principles which, when applied, can help to give children the space in which to express themselves and the confidence to do so. It is important to recognise that children of different ages will have different levels of communication skills. A child of six or seven will obviously communicate very differently from a 15-year-old. Young children may find it easier to talk through puppets or about a drawing they have done or to communicate through role play. Older children often find it easier to interview each other. The principle of "child-to-child" communication which has been developed in health education can also be an effective method of oral testimony collection. Children are often at their most communicative and uninhibited when given a specific piece of action research to do on their own, without an adult present. Giving them the tape recorder and asking them to interview each other or record their songs and stories can be very effective.

Similarly, children often communicate better in groups, and focus group discussions may be a more appropriate forum for collecting children's testimony than the one-to-one interview. If a one-to-one interview is necessary or preferred, it is advisable to conduct it in the presence of what has been termed a "significant adult", one who can support the child and reassure him or her of the purpose of the interview [16]. This might be a parent or an older sibling, or a confidante such as a favourite teacher. Once again, with any interviews relating to human rights abuses or traumatic or painful experiences, it is vital to ensure that there is a "good ending" to the interview, and to provide the child concerned with positive support afterwards. He or she must be encouraged to feel that she has done the right thing by talking, and that there is no need to feel disloyal, guilty or ashamed of speaking out [17].

Preparation and training

Whatever method of interviewing is chosen, a training session for interviewers is an essential part of preparation. Any such session should include clarifying the aims of the project, and discussing and refining the issues to be explored in the light of the local context and the interviewers' own knowledge of it.

Ideally, interviewers should originate from the same area as their subjects or one similar to it, but they will still need familiarisation with the project's subject matter and the issues likely to come up during the "listening" process. One of Britain's pioneering social historians in the 1890s, Beatrice Webb, wrote about the "impertinence" of interviewing people without sufficient knowledge of local practices and terminology, and the main issues concerning people in their daily lives [18]. In some rural development work, for example, this might involve having a basic understanding of local geography, history, kinship and social structures, land tenure, political organisation, gender roles, labour patterns and migration trends. At the same time, interviewers must not be tempted to feel that they already know many of the answers they seek. Their purpose is to learn from someone who is better informed than they are, and who may well have a different perspective on the issues in question.

Familiarity with such contextual information makes for more relevant questioning and helps to establish mutual respect—if the narrator senses that the interviewer is ignorant of the most basic features of his or her lifestyle, this is not conducive to a good relationship. Preparation can also result in a better understanding of what might be left unsaid. This might be because for the interviewee, it would seem to be stating the obvious, or because the form of the question was inappropriate.

Speak for Yourself / Longman Namibia

A leading question presumes the answer.

Too Much respect !
Didnt get enough into question
Needed to question
What we were being told.

questions

concentration, and a genuine commitment
respect the views of others, a crucial
s that of putting questions and guiding
vs should not be straightjackets which force
itural and passive roles as objects of the
ey should be semi-structured but guided
which recognise them as the active subjects of the
interview, free to act as narrator or witness of their own
experience in their own idiom. Interviewers should be aware of
their body language, too: they should make eye contact and
make culturally appropriate gestures to indicate agreement,
enjoyment, sympathy, understanding or encouragement.

The ability to keep an open mind which can respond quickly
to the unexpected and spot interesting and unusual avenues for
further questions is a vital ingredient of good interviewing. An
element of lateral listening is required—looking beyond or
around evasive replies, and "listening between the lines". This
can help to identify what is being left unsaid and to assess the
significance of pauses and silences [19]. Keeping an ear open for
these areas of experience at which the narrator may hint, but
not bring into the interview, is an important part of being open-
minded and creative, and not confining oneself to the straight
line of the narrator's thought. There may be certain areas which
the narrator is wary of discussing or which he or she considers
irrelevant to what the interviewer wants to hear. Imaginative
listening and sensitive but probing questioning can help to
uncover such material and broaden the interview.

Thus, a good interview is semi-structured and
improvisational, and a good interviewer's aim is to say as little
as possible and to listen and learn as much as he or she can.
Good questions are those which make sense to and animate the
narrator; guide the direction of the testimony while giving him
or her plenty of space for self-expression; and ensure that the
necessary topics are covered and all leads, however
unexpected, are followed through.

The golden rule is not to box people in with a rigid set of
questions, but to be flexible within an overall plan. This need
not be a list of specific questions, but rather a logical grouping
of the topics to be covered. Often a chronological sequence is

best. This kind of "interview guide" acts more like a map which shows where the interview is going, but will ensure that it does not drift aimlessly or lose direction when detours are taken.

The shortest questions are usually the best. So-called *open questions* (can you tell me the story of what happened then? how did you feel about that?), which give the narrator scope to expand, should form the basis of an interview. *Closed questions* (did you join the army?), which tend to produce brief answers, are appropriate only when essential information or clarification is needed. *Leading questions* (was that good?) which tend to suggest a specific answer should be avoided. However, in some situations leading questions can be used provocatively—as a *prod* to draw a strong and perhaps contrary reaction (surely, he was the most generous landlord?!). Interviewers should also avoid *double-barrelled questions* which contain two questions in one (how do you make that and where did you learn?). These confuse people and usually mean that one of the two answers is not given.

At various stages in the interview *precision questions*, which require short but exact factual information, will be necessary (what was the name of that market? what year was that?). However, understanding of different modes of cultural expression is vital here: those whose education or training has been Western-influenced may have a desire for specific measurements of time, distance and quantity which is not reciprocated by those being interviewed. Such numerical accuracy may not be relevant to their lives, and the personal or collective time-frame may be measured not so much in dates, months and years as by notable events or periods of time, seasons and other more qualitative characteristics.

Throughout the interview it will also be necessary to *prompt* and *probe* with short questions which encourage the narrator to expand further in one direction (could you tell me more about that?), or to go into greater detail about a subject (could you explain exactly how that system worked?). For prompts and probes to work, it is useful to have a variety of cue words to use (describe, illustrate, discuss, compare, expand). As the unexpected appears, any leads will need to be taken up and detours followed. In order to get back to the main topics or to follow up previous leads, return prompts (earlier you were saying...) will be needed.

Props and mnemonics

Questions are not the only way to inspire a narrator and jog the memory. Physical objects, such as old tools, photographs and traditional costumes or artefacts, can provide the focus for a more detailed testimony or group discussion. A farmer will often be more eloquent when holding an implement and describing its function. A refugee may find much more to say when looking at a picture of home. However, any prop should be carefully chosen, otherwise they will tend to distract the narrator and divert the interview instead of giving it depth.

One prop which is central to the communicative repertoire of Native Americans is the talking-stick [20]. This is a ritual stick which lies in the centre of any group of people who are there to talk or listen, whether it be at a political meeting or a storytelling session. In order to speak a person must go into the centre of the circle and pick up the stick. The speaker must then hold it while they talk and replace it when they stop. The stick places certain responsibilities upon speaker and listeners alike. It requires the latter to listen actively and patiently, but also tends to curb excessive talkativeness on the part of garrulous speakers and gives courage to the shy. Similar indigenous speech rituals should be employed wherever they exist.

Revisiting a place and conducting an interview *in situ* or during a "walkabout" can also free the mind and allow someone to recall the past more easily. Such walkabouts might include: visiting a sparsely wooded watershed which used to be a forest, in order to discuss environmental history and change; returning to a mine or factory which used to be a place of work, to discuss child labour; or examining an abandoned and broken pump, to discuss irrigation techniques and land use [21].

Role play can also be useful as a mnemonic or memory aid, particularly in groups, but also in one-to-one interviews (if you had been the elder what would you have done?). Role play not only releases memory through the re-enacting of situations or events (a certain dance, a typical working day, a particularly important meeting), but also allows people to be less inhibited as they narrate events under the cover of a different persona. Hearing old stories is another good way to jog the memory, and a song or tune from the past can be particularly evocative, taking the mind right back to the time the interviewer is investigating.

Visual techniques

While props and mnemonics help to jog people's memories, some visual techniques may assist them to express the past more clearly. Many oral testimony projects rely on straightforward interviewing alone, but additional visual methods can be helpful when testimony is being gathered among groups unfamiliar with the interview form. Creating a diagram or making a model can take the place of a potentially awkward personal interaction between interviewer and narrator; or may complement, assist or encourage people's verbal performance. Such material can then be displayed alongside the testimony in any report, exhibition or book resulting from a project.

Robert Chambers has described a range of techniques which can be used by rural people and development workers to give expression to various aspects of the past or recent past. These include time lines and biographies (including ethno-biographies); historical maps and models; historical transects; and trend diagrams and estimates [22]. Older people in the community usually play a key role in providing and shaping the relevant historical information in these techniques.

A *time line* is a list of key events, changes and "landmarks" in the past, written up in chronological order on a large sheet of paper. It is often a useful way of putting an individual's or a community's history into perspective by identifying the broad framework of events which shaped their past. It can therefore be a good way into a life story interview or focus group discussion and may also provide the basis for the interview map. Figure 1 (opposite) shows a time line produced by a village in Tamil Nadu, India, stretching from 1932 to 1990 [23].

YEAR	EVENTS	FIG 1
1932	—TANK UNDERTAKEN BY GOVT	
1935–1946	— ESTABLISHMENT OF VERANDA SCHOOL BY GOVT	
1947	— INDEPENDENCE	
1948	— 16 WERE DIED DUE TO CHOLERA, FAMINE	
1954	— ROAD, THATCHED SCHOOL	
1956–1964	— CYCLONE, FLOODS	
1966	— NEW SCHOOL BUILDING	
1968	— AGAIN CHOLERA, 4 WERE DIED	
1970	— ELECTRICITY FACILITY, BRIDGE, 150 FAMILIES MIGRATED BECAUSE OF SEVERE DROUGHT	
1977	— ESTABLISHMENT OF NOON-MEAL CENTER	
1978	— COMMUNITY WELL, 2 BORE WELL FOR DRINKING PURPOSE	
1983	— TINP	
1984	— ELECTION BOYCOTT. ONE MORE BORE WELL . DRINKING WATER OVERHEAD TANK. STREET TAPS BY GOVT	
1984–1985	— NON FORMAL EDUCATION BY GOVT	
1987	— SPEECH	
1989	— GROUP HOUSES FOR 20 HARIJANS	
1990	— HEAVY CROP DAMAGE BECAUSE OF FLOOD	

A visual *biography* is a similar kind of chart which traces the "life" of a particular phenomenon, whether it be a famine, a certain crop or diet, or the development of a kind of technology. These biographies are particularly useful for single-issue histories and can form the framework for the interview.

Maps can be drawn on paper or on the ground with sticks, chalks, pens or paints. Those worked on the ground can be photographed or transcribed on to paper before they are destroyed. Maps of the past are particularly useful in illustrating ecological histories and showing previous land-use patterns, plant and animal coverage. Figure 2 (below) shows the landscape change over the past 25 years in Abela Sipa Peasant Association in Ethiopia [24].

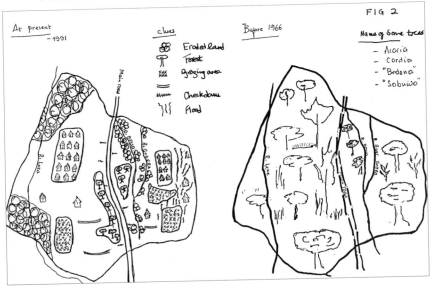

Three-dimensional *historical models* using local materials have aided discussion on erosion and other environmental and agricultural concerns. In another example described by Chambers, villagers from Seganahalli in Karnataka, India, made two models on the ground. One showed their watershed as they remembered it 50 years earlier with trees growing on the rocky hills, and the other as they saw it now, with no trees and serious erosion. The striking difference between the two models began an important debate about what should be done, in which the models were used to present and explore the various options [25]. Thus historical analysis can be the trigger to development debate and it can also be used to generate so-called "dream" models and maps, expressions of people's hopes for the future which can then form the basis of development action. *Historical transects* are another kind of diagram which represent changing conditions through time. Again they have traditionally been used in agro-ecosystem analysis and are usually compiled by walking through an area with some of the older inhabitants and recording their recollections of various conditions at key moments identified by the time line. Figure 3 (below) is a transect through time illustrating land-use trends in a village in East Java [26].

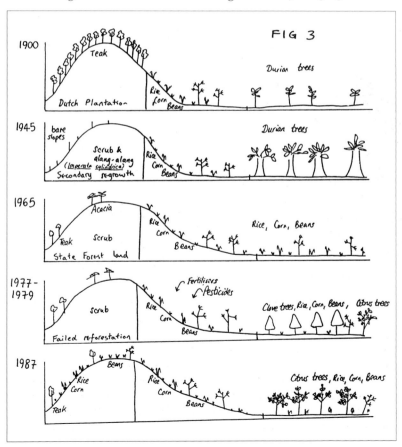

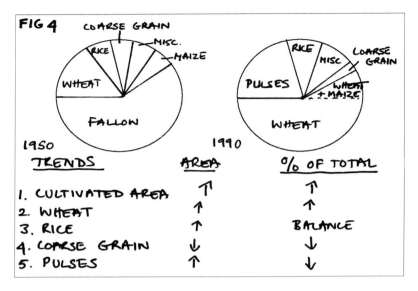

FIG 4

1950

1990

TRENDS   AREA   % OF TOTAL

	TRENDS	AREA	% OF TOTAL
1.	CULTIVATED AREA	↑	↑
2.	WHEAT	↑	↑
3.	RICE	↑	BALANCE
4.	COARSE GRAIN	↓	↓
5.	PULSES	↑	↓

Three main kinds of chart have been used by rural people to estimate or measure change and historical trends: counters, pie charts and straightforward trend lines. Stones, seeds or pieces of stick can be used as *counters* representing absolute or relative values. People can pile up these counters along a simple time line to express absolute values for things like harvest yields, price changes or population changes. They can also place counters in a matrix diagram to express relative values or scores which indicate certain differences over time. For example, one matrix might allow a narrator to express her preferences for certain crops and income-generating activities during five key years in the past.

Pie charts drawn on paper or the ground are another useful way by which people can express relative values and how these changed over time. Figure 4 (above) shows two pie charts made by three elderly farmers which illustrate changing cropping and land-use patterns in a village near Dehra Dun, Uttar Pradesh, India, between 1950 and 1990 [27].

Trend lines are simple graphs in which people use a curved line to illustrate historic trends. A normal histogram or bar-chart can be used for the same purpose. Figure 5 (opposite) shows a trend line drawn in the dust by an old farmer in Mahbubnagar district, Andhra Pradesh, India. The lines illustrate the

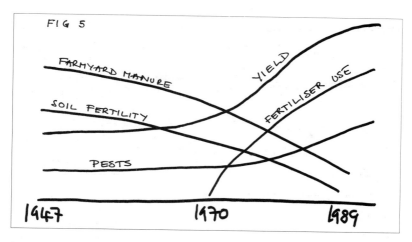

FIG 5

FARMYARD MANURE

SOIL FERTILITY

YIELD

FERTILISER USE

PESTS

1947   1970   1989

increasing and decreasing trends relating to farmyard manure, pests, soil fertility, fertiliser and yields over 40 years [28]. Participatory diagrams are another way in which people can describe a past event and the processes it generated (flow diagrams) or the effect it had on their lives (impact diagrams) [29].

Practice interviews

Any training session should include some practising of interviewing techniques. Working in pairs and using role-play, participants should also gain experience of being interviewed. Each interviewer should then do at least one pilot interview, which they transcribe and, if necessary, translate.

These pilot interviews should be followed by de-briefing sessions in which everyone has a chance to comment on the results and identify areas of interviewing weakness. A good practice session is vital, for listening to a recording or reviewing a transcript will often bring home to the interviewers such things as the need for follow-up questions, the danger of asking too many leading questions, and the problems associated with using concepts which are culturally inappropriate or too abstract to get more than rather superficial responses. This is the time to identify and resolve such communication or cultural difficulties, establish key words and phrases, adjust the interview framework or "map", and refine the particular themes to be explored.

Finally, this is also the time to make sure the interviewers

Project workers in Ethiopia role-play the "insensitive interviewer" and the "monosyllabic informant" as part of their training in interviewing techniques.

understand and fully appreciate the nature and purpose of the project. An interviewer who is under the impression that the aim is primarily to record detailed information and who undervalues the importance of perception as opposed to fact, is likely to become frustrated by or impatient with the discursive nature of an oral testimony interview.

Recording the interviews

Using tape recording equipment involves an element of technical skill and preparation and it is important for interviewers to be familiar with any equipment by practising with it beforehand. Make sure there are enough batteries and find out in advance whether an electricity supply is available. Investment in a battery charger may be worthwhile. Test each piece of equipment immediately before use.

There is a wide range of cassette recorders on the market at a variety of prices. It is always important, whatever your budget, to aim for the best sound quality you can afford. This will determine whether your tapes can be used for radio work, and whether they can be accurately transcribed. The first step is to avoid using built-in microphones, which lower sound quality: so purchase a machine which also has microphone input sockets. The cheapest and most effective external microphones are clip-ons, which will immediately improve the result from any machine. If you can afford a Dolby noise reduction system and stereo input, these add to the quality. It is useful to have a model with a tape counter, especially for transcribing; a battery light; and a built-in speaker as well as the facility to listen to the playback on stereo headphones. It is sensible to test the model you choose in some pilot interviews, before buying any more.

The presence of a tape recorder is always obtrusive to some degree. Some narrators take time to grow accustomed to it; others may be at ease from the start. Giving the interviewee the opportunity to handle the equipment and listen to some playback of their voice at the beginning of the interview can help to break the ice. Some people may find tape recorders unacceptable, particularly when narrating certain events or the more personal aspects of their lives. It is important to be sensitive to this and to establish a policy of switching on and off during an interview. This allows the narrator to say when he or she is covering a particularly sensitive issue and would like the recording stopped. It gives people control over what is "on the record", which may in itself make them feel more relaxed about the process.

After recording, the interview or performance must be preserved. The *master copy* of the tape should be treated as a historical document and never be edited or interfered with. Breaking the two small safety lugs at the top of the cassette makes it impossible to erase or record over the original. Each cassette should then be marked clearly with the interviewee's name, date of birth and a unique reference number, and placed in a secure storage system. The master copies will form the basis of the project's collection or archive. Careful storage of tapes and transcripts is important if the materials are to be preserved over time and readily accessible. The basic points to remember are to keep the cassettes somewhere cool, dry and as dust-free as possible. Avoid touching the tape itself and never store the cassettes in direct sunlight.

Once an interview has been completed, it is important to listen to the recording and write a *summary sheet* which lists the main contents of the interview and notes the date, time and place of the interview, the name of the interviewer, as well as key background information on the narrator. If the facilities are

Seventy eight-year-old Mrs Bryan learning how to use a tape-recorder before becoming an interviewer for the Jamaica Memory Bank.

available, this is a good opportunity to record a ***duplicate copy*** which can then be put into general use while the master is more securely protected, although conditions in the field mean this is not always possible. A photograph of the narrator and of places mentioned in the interview and copies of any diagrams he or she made, could also be attached to the summary sheet.

A system of quick reference ***index cards*** may be a useful alternative to constantly resorting to the longer summary sheets. This could be part of a more detailed ***indexing*** system which also links key subject areas to interview numbers and so allows an element of ***cross-referencing***. For example, a system could identify every interview which mentioned soil conservation practices or child weaning or migration with a simple code (see p133 for more on indexing).

Transcription and translation

The interview should then be transcribed and/or translated to make a written copy. Occasionally, you may be forced by constraints of time or money to transcribe only parts of certain interviews, but it is essential to maintain a high standard when transcribing. The technical quality of the original recording is important at this stage, especially if a playback machine is not available and you are listening through the cassette machine headphones. Being able to work off an electricity supply is also useful; on average it takes five to ten minutes to transcribe every one minute of speech. It therefore requires concentration and patience—and a lot of batteries.

The basic rule of transcription is to render the original speech into written text as accurately as possible by including hesitation, repetition, exclamation, emphasis and dialect. It is important not to correct grammar or word order, or to attempt to make the account read more like a written one. It should remain the spoken word in the style of the narrator, with all the meandering and inconsistencies this may imply. The interviewer or project coordinator should make sure that any references within the text which might not be clear to an outsider—for example, allusions to local dignatories, organisations, cultural events—are briefly explained in notes at the end of the transcript.

Similarly, translation should seek to be as accurate as possible in meaning and style. This can be one of the most difficult aspects of oral testimony work (see overleaf). Some of the issues which arise in translation are related to the general area of interpretation of testimony, which is explored in Chapter Five. Transcriptions and translations should always include figurative speech, such as proverbs and sayings, which should be translated literally, and where they are too culturally specific for others to glean the meaning, followed by an explanation in brackets. For example, the Rundi people of Burundi have a saying that "old women do not whistle without meaning". In their culture, women are forbidden to whistle because it is believed to bring bad luck. But the real meaning of the proverb—and the context in which it is likely to be quoted—is that if someone behaves contrary to tradition, there must be special reasons for doing so. Similarly, the Lunda people of Southern Africa have a proverb: "The impotent man does not eat seasoned food." The literal meaning is that a man who cannot satisfy a woman either cannot find a wife or has one who refuses to cook for him because of his impotency. The social meaning is that those who fail to perform their duties are not entitled to any remuneration.

The trials of translation

Most development projects recording oral testimony are sooner or later faced with the issue of translation. The answers to some key questions—who is to benefit from the project? how is the material to be used? what other audiences do we wish to reach?—will dictate which languages are required and what the translation and transcription procedures should be. A project that aims to influence policy matters may need testimonies recorded in a local language to be translated into both the national, official language (for example, Arabic) and the national, international language (for example, English or French).

Since both transcription and translation are time-consuming processes, the question of how many layers of language are needed becomes very important. In the Sahel Oral History Project (see case study on p126) most tapes were transcribed directly into English or French by the interviewers, on the grounds that there was no immediate use for a written version in the local language, which was anyway preserved on tape. But in the same project, transcriptions have been made subsequently in Soninke (Senegal) and Hausa (Niger), as part of literacy programmes.

Providing the interviewers can speak both the local language and the national language, it makes sense for them to translate the interviews, either from their own transcripts or directly from the tape. But translation is a skilful process, it involves capturing the spirit and flavour of expression as well as recognising the need to interpret the ambiguities of proverbs, or render vernacular names into recognisable equivalents.

In Ethiopia, where SOS Sahel is using oral testimony as part of a research project into food security issues, the complexities of translation are well illustrated. The research was conducted in Wolaitinya, the language of the Wolaita people of southwest Ethiopia. Although the interviewers were fluent in Wolaitinya, they could not transcribe the tapes into the local language because all their schooling had been conducted in Amharic, the national language. The tapes were transcribed directly from Wolaitinya into Amharic, but the project required English versions. As the interviewers were not fluent in English, a second translator had to translate from the Amharic. SOS Sahel decided to have a few of the same interviews translated by two potential translators in an attempt to arrive at the closest and most faithful version. They were both working from the written Amharic and were asked to leave nothing out and to remain as close to the original as possible. Although the extracts below are extreme examples of the divergence in approach, they are by no means unrepresentative of the problems which can arise.

Thus, in answer to the question: Are there species of tree other than eucalyptus?

Version 1: Eucalyptus is most useful. There is also "wanza" but that requires a lot of care and so only a few people have "wanza". Eucalyptus can be planted in soils like this. You can also plant pine but it grows very slowly. Other trees are good for firewood only. A pine like this one makes a good shade. "Zagba" is also very good for shade. Pine has thorny leaves, worst during the dry season. You have got shoes so you don't notice it, but its pricks hurt our children's feet.

Version 2: Eucalyptus is most important. There are other trees as well, for example "wanza" (*Syzigium guinense*). But many farmers do not have these trees. Since the introduction of eucalyptus, the planting of other trees has declined. This is true as far as I can remember. Other trees are used only for firewood. Junipers are used for shade. I have a few junipers. *Podo carpus* is better for shade. Junipers are thorny especially in the dry months; you don't feel it because you are wearing shoes. I don't feel it either now because the ground is wet.

Version 2 gives the Latin names and is more "fluent", but it fails to describe soil conditions, or attribute the lack of popularity of "wanza" to its slow growth. And it has lost the children! Some of the difference of approach in the translation could have been avoided with clearer instructions on, for example, how to translate local names. Different problems are raised in this next example. Question: Are there employment opportunities in the area?

Version 1: Everyone is free to be employed and earn about 3 *birr* a day. But this is good only for people that do not have family responsibility. Otherwise it is better to till the land and feed the family.

Version 2: There are those who are willing to hire their labour and there are those who prefer to till their land. The latter are concerned about their own production so that their families will not be exposed to hunger and famine. The former are usually single, or have no children, or are young men who want to help their families. As for me, I prefer to work on my land. Take, for example, the road rehabilitation where one earns 3 *birr* a day. This is about enough for three days, on the basis of a diet of having one banana a day.

Version 1 fails to distinguish between the motivation and status of wage labourers, and has lost the bananas. Perhaps the translator had grown tired and decided to cut corners. Yet at other points in this particular trial translation the lack of detail in the two transcripts was reversed, illustrating how difficult it is to pick the "best" version.

The translator of version 2 identified a key problem: "The attempt at faithful translation has not been successful because the text was void of much meaning, so I operated on the basis of 'oh, he [the interviewer/transcriber] must have meant this when he wrote that!'. Also, his Amharic is not so good anyway." A university researcher, he produced the most fluent version, obviously editing and smoothing out the rough edges of the original. The translator of version 1 was himself a Wolaitinya speaker. His version was less polished, but on the whole closer to the flavour of the original.

Clearly, to be reasonably confident that there is a "best version" a project has to commit considerable resources both to translating and editing transcripts. Ideally, there should be an original language transcript from the beginning, but even this will be the product of someone one stage removed from the narrator, with the inevitable omissions and confusions. If time is not of the essence, then transcripts/translations should be reviewed against a sample of the original tapes. In practice, given the cost, timing and level of available expertise the transcripts are likely to remain "corrupt"—at best another interpretation. Of course, oral testimony transcripts are likely to be stronger, more genuine examples of individual perceptions than "quotations" filtered through journalists, or consultancy reports. But even oral testimony, in translation, has been filtered. Without access to the original tapes, or a clear statement of translation methods, readers are advised to exercise the usual caution.

Presentation

The purpose behind an oral testimony project will largely dictate the way the material is used and presented. When devising methods of presentation it is important to bear in mind that there will usually be two kinds of audience: the "outside" audience of development workers, donors and policy makers whom the material aims to inform and influence; and the "inside" audience, whose testimony this is and in whose interests it has been collected.

In general terms, oral testimony can continue to be presented in its oral form through audio-visual media, or become part of written work in books or reports. In either of these two media— audio-visual or print—there are six main types of presentation:

- the single life story,
- a collection of testimonies,
- an argued interpretation from testimonies,
- theatre,
- mixed media exhibitions,
- source material.

Whichever is chosen, it is important to ensure that it builds on the comparative advantage of oral evidence and plays to its strengths: on hidden, undocumented worlds; on the reality of family lives, village lives, minority lives; on making connections between sectors which single disciplines can often miss; and on exposing the inadequacy of generalisations and revealing the rich variety of human experience.

The simplest kind of oral history document is the single life story. It can be cut and shaped into an oral work for cassette, radio or TV, or transcribed and edited into a written format. Either way, it can be made into a powerful autobiography. In a collection of testimonies, life stories or relevant parts of them can be grouped together and edited (for cassette, radio, TV or a book) to focus on a particular theme. The editor's skill in comparing and contrasting the material is crucial in giving the collection its shape and message. Equally, the editor can misinterpret or "correct" perceptions. Ideally, although this can be difficult in practice, the edited versions should be checked with the sources.

A single life story or a collection can also be dramatised and presented as theatre. Oral testimony can with skill be turned into compelling drama, raising important issues for actors and audience alike and becoming the occasion for active participation and discussion. Similarly, a mixed media exhibition can be mounted using tape and video "highlights", display boards with transcribed excerpts, artefacts, slides and photographs, and live performances of dance, song and storytelling. Again, the issue of interpretation is crucial, and the "ownership" of life stories used in this way needs to be clear and agreed with the respondents (see p152). Again ideally, plays and shows will be devised by the relevant communities themselves.

Grand Bay Cultural Preservation Project / HelpAge International

Samuel Jarvis performs at a Cultural Gala as part of the Grand Bay Cultural Preservation Project, Dominica. These events, which attract all age groups, have proved a highly popular way for the elders to "return" to the community the wealth of knowledge and skills uncovered and documented by the project.

Research: no room for voices

One of the problems of incorporating oral testimony into development planning is that those who decide on research priorities and funding often have yet to be convinced of the value of actually listening to the voices of people at the grassroots. Or, while they may acknowledge its importance in theory, they design research programmes which in effect prevent such voices from reaching the policy makers.

Deborah Kasente, of the women's studies department of Makerere University, Uganda, faced exactly this frustration when she undertook research into the impact at village level of the Uganda Women's Tree-Planting Movement [30]. The movement was begun by a group of largely middle-class, educated women and was supported by the government, which was under considerable international pressure to demonstrate its commitment to conservation of natural resources. The overriding motivation of the movement, then, was environmental. A major aim was to raise public awareness of, first, the links between an energy and food crisis, overpopulation and the mismanagement of natural resources, and second, of the effects of these on the environment.

Kasente found that the role of the tree-planting movement was perceived differently by those rural women it was designed to serve. On the whole they took part in the movement not for environmental reasons, but for purely economic ones. They planted trees for fuel and timber or to make money from selling seedlings or charcoal. Some appreciated the environmental importance of tree-planting, but most felt such an emphasis reflected the values of the founders of the movement, not theirs. Behind this lay a complex set of economic concerns and priorities and gender relations which needed to be fully appreciated and reflected in the design of such a programme. The neglect of these factors was significant for the outcome: for example, as soon as women who were selling seedlings found their market diminishing, they stopped participating in the programme. After a reasonably healthy start, membership of the movement was falling.

Kasente conducted her research using secondary data (reports of women's groups, seminars and so on), interviews and direct observation. Not surprisingly, it took time to gain the women's agreement to be interviewed: they were extremely busy and had been bothered by such demands before, being in an area which had already served as a research base for other projects. Also interviewed were various people professionally involved with the tree-planting groups. The time and place for interviewing—which for the rural women was usually at lunchtime in their homes—were chosen by the interviewees, some of whom talked for two hours, some for just half an hour. The conversations were conducted in the vernacular and then translated.

When it came to presenting her findings for those who had funded and commissioned the study, Kasente found that the style and structure in which she was expected to write her report meant there was no real outlet for the women's voices. She had to summarise her findings, and quantify the information. "There is a problem with research writing as a discipline. It is quite limiting. I found I had to leave out most of the women's words—the views and perceptions contained in the interviews. There was interesting material which was relevant to the broader issue—that people won't grow trees unless it is both feasible and attractive from their point of view—but it just didn't fit under the neat headings required in the report." Development planners and policy makers need to make research programmes more flexible and to be more willing "to listen" to voices at the grassroots, even if it is only by reading written translations. To do justice to the views of the women, they needed to be presented in the unwieldy yet rich pattern of ordinary speech, not tidied up into short summaries.

These forms of presentation are particularly appropriate for cultural preservation programmes, advocacy and human rights campaigns, development education programmes, or—in the case of single-issue collections—the presentation and dissemination of indigenous knowledge. Theatre and other kinds of oral artistry and performance may also be the most immediate and appropriate ways in which to "return" the material gathered to the community.

These types of presentation aim to let narrators speak for themselves as much as possible. An alternative approach is to put together an argued interpretation, which analyses the material, seeking insights and information, and then develops a particular hypothesis. Quotations may be interwoven with analysis and additional sources to complete the picture. Any maps, models or diagrams made by narrators can also be included and placed with oral testimony, alongside other quantitative information, to complement, confirm or question the testimony. This was largely the approach used in the report on Somalia's immunisation programme, described in the first case study of Chapter Five, and in the "environmental history" of Mazvihwa, Zimbabwe, mentioned in Chapter Three (see p24). Such combinations tend to be the exception rather than the rule, however, and many organisations funding research still favour reports which confine themselves to facts, figures and findings, rather than making space for the verbatim comments of those at the sharp end of development, as Deborah Kasente of Uganda's Makerere University points out in the box opposite.

Oral testimony can also be made available as original source material for development practitioners, researchers, journalists, teachers and others. It can be used to produce literacy and health education materials, training materials for agricultural extension workers, and materials for schools, adult education and development education programmes. The case study on the Sahel Oral History Project in the next chapter points out the value of making such material available to a wide range of audiences, but also the problem of its potential misuse and a "rent-a-quote" approach.

Whatever the difficulties inherent in achieving effective presentation and dissemination of testimony, it is the key to ensuring that ordinary people's views and perceptions begin to exert influence on development staff, governments, donors, policy makers and academics. The collection of testimony is not enough; to listen in order to bring about change means communicating what has been heard to those who can facilitate change. As one mother in Hargeisa, Somaliland, put it at the end of an interview: "That is enough of my miserable situation. It is not words that can change my life, but a change in my country [31]." Words can change lives, but only if people can be persuaded to listen and to act.

CHAPTER FIVE

CASE STUDIES

Why an immunisation programme failed to make its mark on women: Somalia

Anne LaFond

In 1978 the government of Somalia embarked upon an Expanded Programme of Immunisation (EPI). The Somali programme was one of many national initiatives started at that time, part of the global strategy supported by UNICEF and other donors which seeks to achieve universal child immunisation by the year 2000. The EPI programme aims to immunise all children under five against the six killer diseases: diphtheria, whooping cough, tetanus, polio, measles and TB. It also aims to immunise all women of child-bearing age against tetanus to minimise neo-natal deaths of mothers and children. Large-scale immunisation programmes are relatively complicated to administer, involving multiple doses of vaccines and follow-up visits spread over a period of several months.

In 1985, a renewed drive for immunisation got under way and three successive campaigns were held throughout Somalia. These mobilised all levels of government staff and party cadres, but the methods used to ensure compliance were often extreme. The Save the Children Fund (UK) team which studied the immunisation programme recorded that "mothers refusing immunisation were threatened with fines or imprisonment, and health staff also exerted consistent pressure on the community, actively seeking out children whose mothers failed to attend [1]." The campaigns brought about a dramatic increase in coverage: from an estimated 15% to 79% in Mogadishu by 1987, and from 7% to 76% in Hargeisa. When the campaigns ended, however, coverage fell back. While access to immunisation had improved, demand was very low: mothers simply did not present either their children or themselves for immunisation. By 1989, immunisation coverage for some diseases in Somalia had dropped back to around 25%.

At this point the Ministry of Health (MoH) and Save the Children Fund (SCF) teamed up to study the falling demand and try to find out more about why women in particular seemed to have problems with accepting immunisation. Their research culminated in a report entitled "A study of immunisation acceptability in Somalia" [2]. The main part of the research involved the collection of oral testimony, an unusual approach for an official report. Its 88 pages contain 94 passages of testimony, in which people describe in their own words their views and experience of immunisation.

The main objective of the study was "to determine the factors which contribute to immunisation acceptance, and to understand the influence of these factors on health-seeking behaviour". An important secondary objective was to ensure that the study's findings could be easily understood and taken up by MoH managers and staff at all levels. It was felt that ministry staff needed some clear messages from the study with which to redirect their programme, rather than a mass of complex data and statistics.

Methodology
To meet the two main objectives, an oral testimony approach was decided upon. Researchers would explore people's attitudes and behaviour by talking and listening to them; in turn, it was hoped that the testimonies would convey the key issues surrounding immunisation acceptability in an accessible form. The study team selected four communities, two rural and two urban, and devised a methodology involving focus group discussions, interviews with key informants and observation. The research took a deliberately historical perspective and sought to gauge people's experience of immunisation over the 11-year period of 1978-89.

The focus groups brought together between six and 10 people of "like characteristics" in age, sex and socio-economic status (see p68 for focus group methodology). A total of 25 focus group discussions were held. There were three main types of group: mothers (of three different age groups); Ministry of Health staff; and traditional healers and birth attendants. Discussions with mothers were held in the home of one of the participants at an acceptable time, while those with MoH staff were conducted in the clinic after working hours.

Interviews were also held on a one-to-one basis with "key individuals in the community who were in some way associated with the immunisation programme". These included government officials, local representatives of the Somali Women's Democratic Organisation, and government health staff. Key informants were also identified in the community. These included opinion formers and those who advise mothers and influence health beliefs and practice, such as traditional healers and birth attendants, religious leaders (sheikhs and teachers of the Qur'an), grandmothers and fathers. These interviews were undertaken so as to "reveal the broader community dynamics of decision-making and further explore the ideas expressed in the group discussions". Seventy-seven interviews of this kind were held, lasting for between one and three hours, as did most of the focus group discussions.

The final method of research was simple observation. Members of the MoH/SCF team observed vaccination sessions at immunisation sites as well as the curative practices of traditional healers, paying particular attention to the interaction between the various players in each environment.

Field work lasted 12 weeks. The interviews and moderating of focus group discussions were carried out in Somali by a team of two: a male community health nurse connected to the EPI programme and a woman graduate from the MoH statistics department. Both underwent a three-week training programme, during which guidelines were drawn up for group discussions and the one-to-one interviews. These were tested and refined in a pilot study, as a result of which the main topics to be explored emerged as follows:

- awareness and knowledge of immunisation;
- attitudes towards the characteristics of immunisation;
- safety, effectiveness, accessibility and cost;
- perceptions of vaccine-preventable diseases;
- perceptions and practices related to prevention;
- perceptions of methods of immunisation promotion and delivery;
- general attitudes towards health services;
- the role of health advice.

Listening to mothers

The discussions and interviews produced a wide range of testimony. Mothers represented a significant proportion of those interviewed and they spoke of their experience of and attitudes to immunisation. They also described their own beliefs about prevention and protection, which are so central to the concept of vaccination. Many mothers revealed that they had different perceptions of the six diseases: the cause of measles was a mystery, it seemed to be "in the air", so preventing it by immunisation was regarded as no more and no less appropriate than any other approach. By contrast, diseases such as diphtheria and neo-natal tetanus were seen as caused primarily by spiritual forces and therefore were more appropriately dealt with by traditional healers.

The mothers also voiced their anxieties about what they saw as the dangers of immunisation, and their views on which vaccines seemed to work best. Many women spoke with passion about the way in which the EPI programme had been promoted, often by force, and about their fears that immunisation would affect their fertility. They told of how they respected the advice received from family, friends and traditional healers more than that which came from the MoH clinics, in which they lacked confidence.

The majority of women were well aware that immunisation has a preventive purpose, often explaining that it is used "to go before" an illness, and very few confused immunisation with curative treatment. They explained how they already had important protection practices of a religious nature. In the words of one mother: "People cannot do anything. Only Allah has the power to protect. Mostly we use the Qur'an and religious amulets as protection....People in the community tell you to do this."

Because disease was seen to come and go as a result of God's will, the implication was that it could not be predicted or prevented other than by God. This belief undermined the notion of medical prevention as people only concerned themselves with a disease once it had arrived, and doubted the power of drugs to fend off what God ordains. One traditional healer explained:

The advice I give to mothers for themselves and for their

children's health problems is not that of prevention but of
treatment, because only Allah knows what is coming. And also
we are not giving advice about something which does not yet
exist.

Women's testimony revealed that most had received and
understood the information that immunisation is targeted at
children under five, and at women between 15 and 45. But
many were not aware that the protection provided by
immunisation lasts for life, neither had they been fully
informed over the years about the side effects of vaccination,
such as fever, stiffening and aching. They were therefore
repeatedly alarmed by these symptoms, which seriously
undermined their faith in immunisation and were to them an
indication of there being more dangers than benefits in
vaccination.

It became obvious that this lack of communication stemmed
from the way that many of the early EPI campaigns had been
promoted—by force and with minimal explanation. "I was
forced to take immunisation...they took me there by force and
we got immunisation. As a result, my children got fever, cough,
vomiting, diarrhoea and swelling...," said one mother. A
government health worker's testimony reinforced this view:

> *Mothers used to refuse because it was new to them and all the*
> *immunised children got high fevers and some had bad wounds*
> *from the immunisation given in the arm. All this made the*
> *mothers turn against us. They blamed us for forcing them to take*
> *something which made their children sick.*

At the heart of the women's anxiety was incomprehension
about the idea of making a healthy child sick, combined with a
deep mistrust of government motives:

> *Why do you immunise a child and make him sick? It is the*
> *government who brought us immunisation, telling us a lie about*
> *the importance of immunisation. During that time many*
> *mothers escaped. They ran because the child gets sick. They are*
> *refusing because of sickness, the wound and the fever.*

Women explained how concern at the side effects developed
into rumours about the tetanus vaccine given to women of
child-bearing age. Once again, because insufficient information

was given, people were left to draw their own conclusions and many became convinced that the purpose of the tetanus vaccine was to stop population growth rather than to prevent tetanus:

> *In the first place, they told us the younger mothers should come and be immunised and we started asking ourselves questions. Why are they looking for young mothers? Because they are producing children, that's why they give it. The people said once you get immunised you won't be pregnant for four years, so they ran.*

Grandmothers confirmed these rumours and often admitted to being the source of them: "An old lady like me will stand in the line at the clinic and will say to her—you will lose your menstruation and the baby. What can they do? They will run."

Changing attitudes
The women also revealed how their attitudes evolved over the years, as some of their anxieties and suspicions were allayed by experience, if not by improved information from health staff. Women who were immunised against tetanus did get pregnant and children who had been immunised against measles did not get measles. One government health worker remembered how such changes in attitudes came about: "In one village we immunised some of the children and some mothers kept their children away. The measles broke out and killed many children. After that many mothers came to the clinic asking for immunisation. They saw that immunised children did not get measles." This experience was confirmed by mothers and more importantly by grandmothers, who have authority in health matters: "We have not seen an immunised child get measles. Since immunisation came we are resting from this disease....".

Following this change in attitude, women stressed that some of the continuing reluctance to come forward for immunisation was due more to inconvenience than fear of side effects or sterilisation or a lack of confidence in the effectiveness of vaccinations. For many, immunisation was impractical and time-consuming. As one government official explained: "There are some families where both the woman and the man work on the farm and they leave their children at home to care for the other children and no-one can take them to the clinic. There is no time."

But a further factor was the women's lack of confidence in the MoH clinics, rather than in immunisation itself. Because clinics were so poorly equipped and the staff so unsympathetic when providing curative services, women felt no incentive to take their children there on a routine basis and so opportunities for immunisation diminished: "The people in the clinic do not show a happy face; they seem upset by your presence and they do not seem willing. They look you up and down and do not seem happy by your presence. These young girls really do not know anything."

The information MoH staff gave out, especially about immunisation, was also considered grudging and inadequate. Not surprisingly, mothers had more confidence in traditional healers, sheikhs, pharmacies, private doctors, and known and trusted friends and relatives. It was to these people that they turned for most of their information and advice about immunisation, childbirth and child health. "For health advice you ask mothers with more experience than yourself, older mothers with many children who have passed many problems with sickness, mothers in the neighbourhood. These mothers will tell you where to take the child," explained one woman.

Recommendations

After listening to the many people interviewed in the study, MoH and SCF staff were able to recommend major changes in the national immunisation programme. And the first thing the new approach emphasised was the importance of information: any new EPI initiatives should be based on "education rather than compliance". Health education activities had to be designed that recognised the prevailing notions of disease prevention, and included mothers and key opinion formers such as traditional healers, birth attendants, older women and religious leaders.

At field level, supervisors and health workers began to tailor their messages to meet the gaps in women's knowledge and to discuss immunisation in the context of their religious beliefs surrounding protection and prevention. There was a new commitment to involve the community in the promotion of immunisation. Efforts to enlist the active support of traditional health advisors and healers became a central part of the information strategy.

Finally, the report stressed that if modern medicine and immunisation programmes were to be credible to people, the curative services of local clinics and of mother and child health centres would have to be improved. As long as mothers perceived these as ineffectual and uncooperative, immunisation campaigns which were centred around those services would be seen in a similar light and be undermined by association.

Presentation

The study team had met their first objective of understanding people's attitudes and behaviour surrounding immunisation. It also had to meet its second goal: to present these findings clearly and effectively to health planners, policy makers and workers at field level. While the testimony approach was very successful in providing "information which was accessible both intellectually and conceptually to programme managers and implementors", it was recognised that planners and policy makers might not be so easily convinced by such "raw material". The report, therefore, was an attempt to combine the qualitative material of oral testimony with the quantitative forms of information more readily acceptable to planners and policy makers.

People's testimony was interspersed with analysis, summaries, conclusions and recommendations. In addition, the study also presented women's views in more traditionally quantitative formats such as charts and graphs. For example, the different levels of awareness of particular issues were represented in diagrammatic form. And the two graphs opposite were created from the views expressed in the discussions to represent mothers' perceptions of the seriousness of different diseases and the effectiveness of immunisation.

The presentation was deliberately designed to make the report convincing and acceptable to health planners in government, NGO and donor organisations, recognising a tendency to dismiss testimony as purely "anecdotal" and lacking the substance of facts and figures. While allowing people the space to speak and be heard, it also went some way towards presenting their views in formats which were familiar to the professionals it sought to influence. The manner of

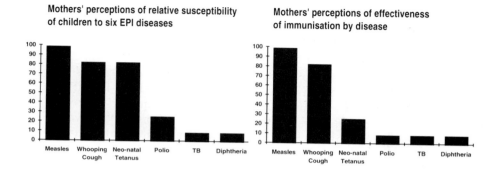

Mothers' perceptions of relative susceptibility of children to six EPI diseases

Mothers' perceptions of effectiveness of immunisation by disease

presentation is crucial if oral testimony is to be accepted by the development establishment. Too often, research proposals are designed in such a way that it can be hard to include the actual testimony of people in the resulting report (see p92).

The results

As Somalia tragically descended into civil war in the months following the study, it has not been possible to assess the impact of the changes to EPI strategy, and it is now impossible to estimate how successful they might have been. Nevertheless, the study is important as a demonstration of how the collection of oral testimony can reveal crucial and previously unrecognised perspectives on a particular issue. The words of the Somali women are lucid and direct. They represent the firm voice of experience and provide a counterpoint to the uncertain assumptions of other people speculating on their behalf. They show how data and statistics alone can present only a partial picture. The improved understanding of the perceptions and experiences which influence the take-up of immunisation provided a more solid starting point for redesigning the information, education and extension components of the EPI programme, and for respecting and involving women much more fully throughout the whole process.

Community history and mobilisation: Recife, Brazil

Paul Thompson

Today a city of two million, the metropolis of Brazil's vast northeast, Recife straddles a river estuary where Brazil juts farthest into the Atlantic Ocean: close to the equator, nearest to Africa. The Portuguese settlement of Brazil, from 1500 onwards, began from this coastline. Behind the reefs and palm-fringed coastal beaches those first European colonists found a dense tropical forest, the Mata Atlântica, sparsely populated by Indians. A hundred kilometres inland, beyond a range of hills, was a drier, less densely wooded interior, the *sertão*. In the centuries which followed, the region developed a double economy. Along the coastal strip, where the soil is rich and rainfall high, the forest was cleared for sugar plantations, worked largely by slave labour imported from Africa until emancipation in the 1880s. It was on the sugar trade that the Portuguese monarchy depended for its cash revenues, and politically the sugar planters always had the upper hand. Recife fed on the trade to become a wealthy merchant city, a centre of fashion.

Beyond the hills, the immense dry hinterland of the interior was colonised by cattle farmers, who used a largely *caboclo* workforce, interbred from poor whites and Indians. Barely scratching a living, they forged a strikingly independent, creative culture with bandit heroes celebrated in *cordel* broadsheet poems and the spontaneous and competitive oral poetry of the *repentistas*, along with craft traditions in textiles, leather and pottery.

Contemporary Recife draws its population from all these elements. The European-descended rich are concentrated principally in the southern suburb of Boa Viagem, as well as in patches of older neighbourhoods elsewhere. The historic city centre is now made up of offices, warehouses, shops and markets, with only a few permanent residents. It is circled by neighbourhoods with very varied housing, which have grown especially rapidly in recent decades: Recife was a town of little more than 100,000 in the 1900s, reaching half a million by the late 1940s, and quadrupling again since then. This great influx into the city has been attracted partly by the work which it offers, in manufacturing as well as commerce, but the northeast today is an area of industrial decline rather than growth. The most powerful motivation for migration has been not so much the pull of the city as the push out of the countryside.

In the sugar belt, the land is almost exclusively exploited for the main cash crop, with little space for gardens or smallholdings, so that there is nothing to sustain those who are not directly employed and the work itself is seasonal. In the interior the living was always poor. The *sertão* has been subject to periodic droughts lasting several years since at least the early eighteenth century: very likely in part reflecting a man-made climatic change brought about by the felling of the coastal forest. Thus most of Recife's migrants were fleeing intolerable rural poverty. Recent studies suggest that the northeast accounts for more than half of all Brazilians living below the poverty line, with incomes of less than $50 monthly. The regional infant mortality rate is around 8%, and there is evidence that in the drought areas and also in the city slums, the average height of adults is declining [1]. The poor of Recife live in *favelas*, shanty towns of makeshift huts, patched together from wood, cardboard, corrugated iron and straw, on the land least sought for better housing: the steeper hillsides, and the river banks and salt-marshes. The more recent *favelas* have mud streets, intermittent or no electricity and water, and inadequate drainage. Some of the houses extend over the sea estuary, perched on stilts in the tidal mudflats.

While the *favelas* of Recife are similar in origin, their evolution has differed strikingly. Many have remained locked in a vicious circle of unsanitary conditions and social disorganisation. Others have been transformed into streets of small colour-washed houses, solidly constructed in masonry with tiled roofs, sometimes with gardens. Some streets even have newly planted trees. This evolution has been the result of a collective neighbourhood process which has combined locally sustained self-improving activities with political demands for basic services and, most fundamentally of all, for recognition of the inhabitants' right to the land they have occupied.

Undoubtedly, numerous factors contributed to success in each case: the local economic context, the original ownership of the land, as well as political and religious influences. Two

Recife working-class neighbourhoods which originated as
favelas are best known, not only in the city but throughout
Brazil, as models of the struggle for self-improvement: Casa
Amarela and Brasilia Teimosa. In each of them a sense of
common identity, and also of moral justice in the
neighbourhood's claims, seems always to have been
fundamental, and a crucial strand within this has been the
development of a local historical tradition.

Casa Amarela: mobilisation from myth

This local historical tradition does not have to be true to be
powerful, as Casa Amarela shows. It is much the larger of the
two communities: a group of about eight neighbourhoods
clinging to the steep and once densely wooded slopes of the
first foothills inland from Recife. Up to the early twentieth
century the site was virtually uninhabited, and the real
population influx and settlement did not begin until the 1940s,
continuing from then, with both individual squatting and
collective occupations of woodlands, into the 1970s and 1980s.
Its population today is well over 200,000.

For the people of Casa Amarela the most crucial battle has
been for the right to the land, and it was finally won only in the
1980s. A sense of justice founded on a new myth was the
cornerstone of the local struggle. This was why they called it
"The Movement of Nobody's Land". It is not clear who were
the real owners of the hills before the 1940s, but they may have
belonged at one stage to a former sugar plantation, which had
its own chapel of São Pantaleão. The local Rosinho family
claimed to be heirs to the plantation, and in 1945 set up an
estate agency which began to claim and in many cases collect
rent from the settlers. But the local population maintained an
alternative story: that São Pantaleão had formerly been the
chapel of a religious order, now dissolved, whose aged last
brother had given the land to its occupiers before returning to
Portugal.

There were no documents to back this tradition: it was
popularly believed that they had been destroyed in a flood and
that the papers held by the Rosinho family were forgeries. But
certainly, in the long battle for possession of the land from the
1960s onwards, the local conviction that the occupiers had a

historic right to their own land was a fundamental rallying force. As one of the first rent refusers put it: "[Rosinho] wasn't and isn't the proprietor. That's the history. It's a theft, a robbery."

Casa Amarela today has an exceptionally well-coordinated and vigorous associational life, conducted at a local level but brought together through the Federação das Associações, Centros Comunitários e Conselhos de Moradores de Casa Amarela (FEACA), its federation. In the *bairro* of Morro da Conceição, for example, there are groups concerned with land rights, education, health, public cleanliness campaigns, milk distribution, drainage and paving, public security (to combat the rising violence caused by economic depression), and women's rights (to spread information on health and sexuality, and to combat *machismo* and domestic violence). Volunteers run street meetings, a local "radio" (in fact a loudspeaker), and a soup kitchen for the very poorest, as well as alternative community schools for both children and adults.

The neighbourhood council of Morro, the Conselho de Moradores, which acts as the coordinating focus of these activities, was first set up in 1980 as part of a well-orchestrated local campaign for water supplies. But unlike most associations thrown up by specific political campaigns in Brazil, it did not disappear when the campaign itself ended. Undoubtedly, local organisational activity, centred around an annual religious festival, together with the backing of a radical priest, helped to sustain it. But again, a sense of local history has been a crucial source of confidence. Thus the Conselho marked its own tenth anniversary in 1990 with a special week-long programme celebrating "the years of history and struggle".

There were meetings on women's issues and campaigns for improved housing, education and health, as well as

Conselho de Moradores do Morro da Conceição "10 ANOS DE HISTÓRIA E LUTAS"

Autor: CASSIMIRO ROCHA JUNIOR

a photographic exhibition, a football match, a triumphal dance, and a mass in the parish church. A *cordel* broadsheet was also published with a poem by Cassimiro Rocha, a local poet. In a manner typical of local artistry, this gave detailed verse accounts of the campaigns within a rhetorical framework acknowledging both collective solidarity and divine support:

> *To tell a history*
> *Of struggle and suffering...*
> *I pray the Immaculate Virgin*
> *To intercede with God...*
> *In the midst of Christ's Passion*
>
> *The people cried out for water...*
> *The people were organising themselves,*
> *To destroy the shark...*

In Casa Amarela the establishment of a formal oral history project was thus the confirmation of a local sense of historical identity, rather than a first step in creating one. In 1986 the leaders of FEACA began discussions with the university historian Antonio Montenegro, which resulted in the setting up of FEACA's own Memory Department, for which 100 interviews with local men and women were carried out over a period of a year. The informants were chosen by FEACA, and those who were subsequently included in publications received shares of the royalties. The Memory Department now constitutes a small archive holding the tapes and transcripts, the tapes of six subsequent radio programmes on local history, and a series of photograph albums. These are available to selected researchers. A video and two books have also been published.

The archive is undoubtedly a rare and precious resource, especially for outside researchers in local working-class history and community development. Nevertheless, it is perhaps most significant as a symbolic resource. Its use is inevitably limited in a community with a high illiteracy rate. And although the question of title to the land could possibly recur, since the Ronsinho family were not finally bought out by the state until 1988, the state's decision was the outcome of the political campaign rather than a conversion to the local version of history: so that in legal terms the oral "documents" held by the

Memory Department have little potential value. What matters most is quite simply that the community has made, and holds, its own record.

The Department itself is reluctant to allow too open an access to its material, partly from a fundamental apprehension that it might be misused. This appears to be a typical dilemma in such projects. Here it is hardly surprising, since as recently as 1979 the Morro information centre was so disapproved of by the authoritarian regime that it was raided and closed by the police. Among the documents they seized was a *cordel* poem written by the local priest who as a result was tried and served some months in prison. Democracy is new in Brazil and this makes for considerable caution in the control of archives and information centres. Indeed, another project in São Paulo, which was set up to record local struggles for a health centre, has failed to produce a public archive of any kind: the local council has insisted on holding it privately. The more unstable the political context of a project, the less likely it is that a genuinely open public resource may result.

Even the publications from the Casa Amarela programme have a local value which is more symbolic than practical. One book consists of extended extracts from three life stories, which require considerable commitment as well as literacy to follow through. There is also an illustrated book of briefer extracts, which has proved of some direct use in adult literacy classes in the alternative schools. But it is less suitable for work with younger children—and in this it contrasts with the oral history project in Brasilia Teimosa, which was specifically designed and funded by the Ministry of Education as a school project.

Brasilia Teimosa: history and community identity in schools

Brasilia Teimosa is a smaller community, with some 40,000 inhabitants, and its historical tradition is also shorter. It lies directly across the estuary from the city's centre, at the far end of Boa Viagem's long and luxurious Atlantic beachfront. Originally the beach gave way to a sea wall built on the line of the reefs and protecting the estuary harbour from storms. As the fishermen now recall it: "This here was all sea. We used to come in with the rafts here where the colony is." From the

1930s, however, the dumping of silt from dredging operations in the estuary led to the building up of a triangular spit of land behind the sea wall, to which the Navy claimed ownership. This was the site of Brasilia Teimosa.

First to settle the new land was a colony of fishermen, and they remain the community's historic heart, their boats beached in the pools behind the reefs closest to Boa Viagem's luxury apartments. The development potential of the site they occupy must have been evident from early on. However, their settlement was protected by the Navy, who regarded their presence as valuable since it provided a form of unofficial and unpaid coastguard service.

In the 1950s, however, the land began to be "invaded" by new migrants from the rural hinterland. At first both the fishermen and the Navy strongly resisted, denouncing the new occupiers and calling in the police to destroy their mud-floored, straw-roofed huts. A sustained and organised struggle ensued, with the occupiers rebuilding at night the huts which the police were demolishing by day. In the words of Pelopidas Silveira, ex-mayor: "The invasion was going on in a very organised way. There were 'squatters' who were demarcating streets, defining small lots, building wooden huts and selling them."

Eventually, however, the fishermen were won over by being given full control of a defined area around their colony. After a series of fights with the police and demonstrations outside the city hall, the mayor decided in 1958 to withdraw the city police and accept the occupation. Finally, the Navy withdrew the military police.

In this initial political fight a crucial factor was again the occupiers' belief that the land had no owner. They believed they had a natural right to it because, in the spirit of Genesis itself, it was land which had arisen from the sea. In the words of one witness: "This land was formed by fish that die, by woods, and natural things: so this land does not have any owner, it belongs to all who live in it [2]."

When the mayor of Recife accepted this argument and withdrew the city police, the battle for Brasilia Teimosa was half-won. The neighbourhood in fact took its name from this initial victory: *teimosa* means stubborn, and the allusion to Brasilia came from the construction of Brazil's new capital in the same years. But the mayor's announcement, "I am with you, carry on the fight", did not settle the question; it was more a tolerance of the occupation than a recognition of ownership. Over the next 20 years the community fought off a series of threats, from a proposed yachting marina to a complex of luxury hotels, the latter development put forward by the city hall itself.

In the meantime, the community developed its own self-improvement schemes, often with crucial help from its first priest, Father Jaime. These included the setting up of a residents' council in 1966, mothers' clubs, a church school, health centres, a theatre group and a fishermen's cooperative. Most notably, in 1978 a city proposal for redevelopment, which would have displaced many of the occupants, was defeated after scores of street meetings. A revised urban scheme was implemented, with the city purchasing most of the land but not, significantly, giving legal ownership to the occupants.

The Brasilia Teimosa oral history project arose from a specifically educational initiative linked to two of the neighbourhood's primary schools and carried out in 1982-86. The objective was to promote interaction between the primary schools and the community, and through this to encourage an approach to education which was rooted in local realities. For Brazil, this was a novel idea: traditional teaching has been very abstract, with no reference to social conflict or to the crime, poverty, unemployment and housing difficulties which are part of everyday experience for most working-class children. Similarly, history is taught as the story of national political elites, rather than of local struggles and changes.

The educational project had already resulted in much discussion and many practical experiments, such as the creation by the children of a school "museum of the sea", when it was decided to experiment with the collection of local oral history. The idea was suggested by Ana Dourado, then a history student at the university, and subsequently coordinator of the oral history project from 1985 to 1987. The team also included a university educationalist and two teachers from the schools.

The culture of the fishermen remains fundamentally an oral one, in terms of the transmission both of skills and of history. Many of the older spokesmen were illiterate, but the project was designed to involve as many people as possible as "historians". Some of the women residents became interviewers, while a key role was played by Salviano de Souza, founder of the Fishermen's Union and president of the fishing association. Born in 1918, he had begun fishing at the age of 12, and had a rich and vivid memory. Although unable to write, he loved talking: he was not only interviewed, but went many times to the school to talk to the children for the project—and has continued to do so since. Above all, the children themselves were involved. Indeed, the principal outcome of the project was a school book in which many of the stories and all the illustrations were produced by the children themselves.

The project encountered two principal difficulties. The original intention had been to base it at the school next to the fishermen's association. But when the project team arrived with its new ideas about education, calling for a curriculum which reflected the everyday reality of life in a fishing family, the school's director reacted with hostility, denouncing the team's approach as subversive. Although many of the teachers supported the project, its base had to be transferred to a smaller school, where the teachers were involved in local political activity and the director was more sympathetic to experiments with the curriculum.

Once this initial difficulty was overcome, the project team began working with the children, bringing in Salviano and other older fishermen to talk to them, and then getting the children to draw and tell stories. This generated such a mood of discussion and debate in the community about education, history and popular culture that eventually the teachers in the first school started a movement for the removal of their director. After some months they succeeded, and from then onwards the project worked from both schools.

The second difficulty was more fundamental. Once the process of evaluating the interviews had started, it became clear that there were competing local oral traditions. Different sections of the community held different versions of history, which were in some respects distinctly antagonistic. Thus the fishermen typically considered "us" to be synonymous with the community. They saw themselves as its founders, "owners of the place", who had generously allowed space for "them", the other settlers. Their way of looking at the past was essentially paternalistic, both in their relationship to the other residents (who outnumbered them overwhelmingly), and in relation to the state authority—in gratitude for the protection they had received from the Navy. Their memories contrasted with those of the majority of settlers, chiefly migrants from rural poverty, who had secured their land and improved it only through organised political struggles: for tenure, for electricity, transport, street paving and so on. They, in particular, felt hostile to those older inhabitants who had never joined these struggles: "One cannot talk to somebody who has always stayed in his home. Someone like that didn't make history, he vegetated all his life. He didn't participate [3]."

The team decided to include the perspectives of both the fishermen and the rural squatters in the published material. But a still more explosive issue concerned the local prostitutes, who had also been there from the early days: indeed, most of them belonged to fishing families. Brasilia Teimosa's red light district was already active in the 1940s, when US servicemen patronised the bars closest to the harbour. Few interviews, however, made any mention of the prostitutes. This was an aspect of the neighbourhood's past and present about which, because it seemed to them shameful, informants preferred to keep silent. There was one important exception, Salviano himself, who made a remarkable statement linking the prostitutes and the fishermen:

> Wherever there is a fishing colony, there is also a red light district. Fishermen and prostitutes are the two classes disregarded by the world, which looks down on both of them. And they are both exploited classes, because the fisherman can't name the price of his fish, it's the profiteer who prices it, nor can the prostitute price her own flesh. After the man has slept with her he stands up, and then it's he who decides how much he will pay her.

The entire draft of the school book, including Salviano's statement, was presented to a large meeting of residents. This was a lively occasion with much argument, but the final decision was unanimous: publish everything. Some months later, however, when the book had been published and was in use in the schools, a group of fishermen who had not been at the meeting began to protest against their children using a book which contained such statements. The team held a further well-attended community meeting, which not only reaffirmed the original decision, but resulted in substantial additional

PRODUÇÃO
ALTERNATIVA

BRASÍLIA
TEIMOSA

2ª EDIÇÃO

testimony. Some of this new material has now been incorporated into a second edition of the school book, and its example has been followed in the neighbouring quarter of Pina, originally an island settled by fishermen and dockworkers [4].

Meanwhile, the new edition of *Brasilia Teimosa* continues to be used with enthusiasm in the neighbourhood's primary schools. The teachers work in dark, poorly equipped, crowded classrooms with almost no financial resources for materials. Each classroom is used every day by four different shifts of children, for four hours each. The younger teachers are often untrained students. Nevertheless, they are insisting on a democratising and child-centred approach to education, in which children's understanding begins with their own world and moves outwards. They use the book as an inspiration, along with the 10-minute video which was also produced by the project, and from this starting point move on to talks by Salviano and other older fishermen. The children are then encouraged to create their own materials, partly through interviewing their grandparents and older uncles and aunts. The children then discuss their material in groups of six, and each group selects a story to relate to the whole class. Thus they see the book not as a "dead" object, but as an example to emulate.

There can be little doubt of the project's success in educational terms, and in this respect it is a model which would be well worth following in many other contexts. But the project has proved much more than this. The book helped to crystallise local pride in the past as an inspiration for the continuing struggles of the present. In the six years since its publication in 1986, further successful campaigns have been fought to complete the surfacing of the streets, improve local transport, connect every house with the mains water supply, start a free milk service at the health centre, and rehouse families who were still living in huts on stilts next to the sea wall.

Most fundamental of all, in 1987 a mass campaign was launched to demand legal ownership of the land by the occupiers themselves. In 1989 this crucial step was finally agreed by the mayor of Recife. It seems clear that the strengthening of local pride and the sense of history and identity brought about through the oral history project were in themselves important factors in launching and sustaining this crowning victory of Brasilia Teimosa: a *favela* precariously established on dredged silt, which has transformed itself into a secure, popular neighbourhood.

Both the Brasilia Teimosa and the Casa Amarela oral history projects were short-lived, of no more than two years' duration in each case. There was never time to develop the much fuller and more sustained use of the material collected which has been so successful in many European local oral history projects. These examples do, however, point strongly both to the key role that an alternative sense of history can play in the mobilisation of a community for self-improvement, and to specific forms of educational project work designed to encourage a community's consciousness and sense of identity through a history of common struggle [5].

Documenting traditional environmental knowledge: the Dene, Canada

Martha Johnson

For thousands of years, the environmental knowledge of indigenous peoples around the world has enabled them to utilise the natural resources of their local environment in an ecologically sustainable manner. Only in the past decade has this knowledge—variously labelled as folk or ethno-ecology, traditional environmental knowledge (TEK), indigenous knowledge and customary law—been recognised among the Western scientific community for its value to contemporary environmental management. Today, a growing body of literature attests not only to the presence of a vast reservoir of information regarding plants and animals, but also to the existence of effective indigenous systems of natural resource management.

At the forefront of this burgeoning field of research are indigenous peoples, who are demanding primary involvement in the direction of studies which serve their needs. "Participatory" or "action" types of research have become the accepted approaches to the study of TEK, in which the host indigenous community participates directly in the design and implementation of the project, receives training to allow it to administer and conduct its own research, and retains control over the results. Outside agencies or individual researchers may collaborate with the community, but their role is to provide technical advice and administrative support.

The Traditional Environmental Knowledge Pilot Project of the Dene Cultural Institute, Canada, is one example of a participatory action research project [1]. Starting in mid-1989, a team of local Dene researchers, a biologist and an anthropologist developed methods to document the TEK of the Dene people of Fort Good Hope and Colville Lake in the Northwest Territories of Canada. Over the next two years, information was gathered about the behaviour of different animal species and the traditional rules that governed Dene use of natural resources. The ultimate goal of the research is to integrate Dene TEK and Western science in order to develop a community-based natural resource management system.

The pilot project has only begun to uncover the wealth of ecological information available and to understand the traditional system of environmental management. Most of the information gathered has been concerned with animal ecology: seasonal habitats, feeding habits, relationships and interdependence between different species, life histories, migrations and movements, population cycles and responses of animals to alterations in their habitat.

The nature of Dene traditional environmental knowledge

At the heart of the TEK of the Dene in this part of the Northwest Territories is a spiritually based moral code or ethic that governs the interaction between the human, natural and spiritual worlds. It encompasses a number of general principles and specific rules that regulate human behaviour towards nature, many of which find parallels in other indigenous cultures.

The fundamental principle of the traditional Dene environmental ethic is that the land and its resources should be taken care of for the benefit of future generations. Ensuring that this happens is the responsibility of every individual in the community, as one community researcher explains:

> *Everyone takes responsibility for what's going on, in the land and with the animals—not only the game officers. This is why our system works....Anyone in the community that doesn't follow it, is considered naive and isn't respected in the community. So there is great social pressure when these rules are not followed because our survival depends on the land and animals [2].*

For the Dene, the human, natural and spiritual worlds are tightly interwoven. As in many other indigenous cultures, the Earth is viewed as a living organism. Everything, human, natural and spiritual, has its place in the cycle of life and interference with any component, no matter how small, is bound to have negative repercussions on the other components.

In many instances there is reference to a higher power, the Creator, who ensures that overall order is maintained in the system. Environmental events are often caused or influenced by spiritual forces. Humans do not have any special power or authority over other life forms, and humans and animals have a reciprocal relationship. Animals are available for human use, and humans in turn are expected to treat them with dignity and respect. Similarly, animals in the wild should not be held in captivity and humans should not interfere with their natural habitat or behaviour.

In addition to the general principles and rules of the traditional system of management, which relate levels of harvesting to individual and community requirements (in essence "never take more than you need"), the Dene have developed a number of strategies to ensure the continued existence of healthy populations of the resources they depend on. All these practices are founded on empirical understanding of population dynamics and ecological linkages.

The Dene believe that continued hunting and trapping of animals is important to achieve a sustainable, productive harvest, but also that an area should be left alone for a period of time to allow the population to renew itself. Another common practice is to hunt only the mature animals and leave the females when they are pregnant or caring for young ones.

The Dene have not escaped the impact of modern technology and Euro-Canadian culture. One of the greatest concerns voiced by the elders interviewed in the project is the loss of TEK and cultural values among the younger generation. As one elder explains:

> *The young people today that hunt with skidoos [motorised sledges] seem to shoot more than they need. Long ago when we used to hunt, we always just shot what we needed. They have to learn that's not the way to hunt. A few of them get carried away when they are hunting with skidoos [3].*

Another, younger hunter from Colville Lake reaffirms this concern:

> *The elders are the only ones that can talk to these young men. If a young person isn't taught the proper way to hunt, how will he learn to respect the land or wildlife? They need to be taught. All our elders here in Colville Lake give us, the young people, clear instructions on how to live and use wildlife. The animals are put on this land for our survival....The message has always been in*

our legends that the animals have to be respected. And everyone that uses this land, the Dene and the oil companies will have to learn to respect this [4].

A number of project informants had witnessed changes in populations of wildlife and river fish which they attributed to such factors as industrial development and oil exploration. However, because of time constraints this part of the research was not pursued in greater detail. Nevertheless, it is clear that TEK may be particularly important for evaluating the impacts of industrial development and modern technology on the local environment. For instance, local people are often the first ones to notice any change in the movements of an animal or in the quality of its meat. Since their cultural and economic survival depends upon the continued existence of these natural resources, it is in the best interest of the Dene to ensure that they are used in an environmentally sustainable manner.

The methodology

The research team consisted of three community researchers, chosen primarily on the basis of their fluency in English and North Slavey (the Dene language in which the project was to be conducted), their knowledge of Dene culture, previous research experience, and interest and motivation. Initially, all three researchers happened to be women, but when one of them was unable to continue, she was replaced by a man. It was recognised that it was better to have both men and women as part of the research team to have both views represented. As one of the most experienced researchers pointed out, it took time for her, as a young woman gathering information in a traditionally male domain, to establish her credibility and gain the confidence of some of the male elders.

Two outside researchers, a social scientist and an experienced biologist, trained the community researchers and worked with them for some of the time. They provided a Western scientific perspective and helped to ensure that specific ecological and biological information was collected. They also acted sometimes as "outsiders" in the most useful sense, picking up when questions were required which the community researchers had deemed unnecessary—because to them the answer was "too obvious" or such an integral part of their cultural understanding as to be "common knowledge". Time constraints prevented the outside researchers from observing or participating in traditional activities, which meant the transfer of knowledge was rather one-way. The lack of such first-hand experience may well lead an outside researcher to make incorrect assumptions about the value of information or the way that it is used.

On the other hand, the actual training was as much a learning process for the outside researchers as it was for the "students". It became clear that any training programme had to be very flexible to meet the needs of the community researchers, whose formal education, command of English and experience of the subject matter varied widely. The sessions produced many useful insights into the best methods of teaching the principles, concepts and terminology of social science research and ecology to adults with limited formal education and no scientific training.

With guidance from the Dene Cultural Institute and a Steering Committee made up of six elders, the research team designed and tested semi-structured questionnaires. The Steering Committee was to guide the research team in the subjects to be covered, assist in the interpretation of the findings, and publicise the project within the community. In retrospect, the Steering Committee was not used as effectively as it might have been. Although these elders were very supportive of the project and provided thoughtful insights and information about the history of the region and traditional life, they played only a limited role in the research design and the interpretation of the results. Most decisions regarding the methodology and interpretation of the data were made by the outside researchers in consultation with the community researchers and the Dene Cultural Institute. The research team recommended that future projects establish an Elders' Advisory Council, to assist in the interpretation and analysis of the data throughout the study. More active involvement in the training programme—in the classroom and in the field—would also ensure that the Dene perspective was more formally integrated into the training process.

The primary method of data collection was the interview, using a structured conversational approach. Some cultural bias was inevitable given that questions were initially formulated largely by the outside researchers—who knew what they wanted to "collect" from a scientific perspective—and were then translated into North Slavey. Local researchers were, however, able to exclude anything they felt unsuitable or to include questions of their own design.

The review of the transcript of the test questionnaire revealed many superficial answers and it was revised accordingly. Leading questions were removed, the sequence of topics was re-organised and suggestions from the various advisors were incorporated. The review identified a need to avoid the use of abstract English words and concepts (for example, "evaluation" and "numerical"), some of which were hard for the community researchers to understand, being primarily Western concepts, and all of which were difficult to translate into North Slavey.

Different approaches
On the whole, Western scientists stress the use of quantitative measures while the traditional Dene harvester is more concerned with qualitative information. For example, Western scientists gather quantitative data to build mathematical models of population dynamics, which are then used to calculate the sustainable yields of a resource. The Dene harvester is more interested in conditions in general or in trends than in precise numbers and averages. In addition, the Western researcher and the Dene hunter also often have access to different types of information, and as a result may come to different conclusions regarding a specific problem. For example, in estimating a beaver population the scientist may conduct an aerial count of the beaver lodges in a particular area and multiply this by an assumed average number of occupants per lodge, thus arriving at a certain population estimate. The Dene hunter, on the other hand, knows from his own and other hunter/trapper observations that the food supplies have been depleted in the survey area and that many of the lodges are empty or contain no young beaver. His estimate of the population would therefore be much lower than that of the game manager.

The community researchers also found that questions suggesting control of a species often elicited a negative reaction from informants because of the unfavourable connotation that the idea of controlling wildlife has in Dene culture. Similarly, informants were sometimes reluctant to divulge specific numbers of animals harvested. The community researchers explained that this was because some Dene considered discussion of hunting or trapping success to be bragging, or feared the information might be used against them by the government.

After a second set of interviews was completed using the revised questionnaire, many of the responses were still disappointingly superficial. It was felt that the problem was the question and answer format. By constantly firing questions at an informant, the researchers felt they were restricting his or her freedom to address other issues which were of personal importance. Moreover, it was not clear to what extent the information gathered in this way represented a Dene as opposed to a Western perspective of the subjects being investigated. For many traditional Dene, the Euro-Canadian pattern of question-answer is an alien form of communication. The accepted pattern, for the Dene as well as for many aboriginal peoples, "involves long monologues where questions are answered indirectly and at great length [5]".

After much discussion, it was decided that a more open approach to questioning was needed, and that the questionnaire should serve merely as a checklist for the types of information being sought. Researchers were to allow the information to flow as naturally as possible and not to worry about the order in which topics were covered; the informant was to be free to decide which subjects were important to talk about and how best to present the information.

It was also found that using specific local examples helped make the questioning more relevant. For example, when seeking information about the habitat of a certain animal, it helped to ask the informant to describe the physical characteristics of his trapping area. Equally, it proved hard for people to describe plant species in detail without reference to the real thing. One elder who had been unable to distinguish between different species of willow during the interview, then took the researcher on a tour in which he gave accurate details of several different species of shrubs and trees, and described their value to the wildlife and the local people.

A continuing problem was the inherent contradiction of

seeking to categorise, in terms that are relevant and comprehensible to Western science, the "facts" of TEK. Much traditional knowledge is transmitted in the form of stories and legends using metaphors and sophisticated Dene terminology, which were not always well understood by the younger interviewers, let alone outsiders. One community researcher frequently commented on the elders' use of "hidden words": North Slavey terms and metaphors which were indirect references to certain animals or their behaviour that could not be translated literally into English.

This had implications for translation and interpretation, which ideally needed someone who possessed both a familiarity with the subtleties of Dene stories, metaphors, terms and concepts, and the ability to extract ecological data from the narrative. Where the community researcher did not have sufficient understanding of the former, they could work with an elder, assisted by an interpreter fluent in English. Even more difficult was finding scientific terminology which accurately reflected the indigenous concepts being described.

Integrating Dene TEK and Western science

Despite the preliminary status of the pilot project's findings, it has already revealed some of the important differences and similarities between Dene TEK and Western science and the difficulties of integrating the two knowledge systems. All parties appear to agree that the integration of TEK and Western science is desirable given the need to produce a more complete understanding of the environment and to respect the cultural diversity of the Canadian North. Yet while there has been considerable discussion and a few attempts to establish co-management institutions, the application of Dene TEK at the decision-making level of resource management has yet to be fully realised.

This whole issue is made more urgent because of the gradual disappearance of Dene TEK due to the death of elders and the lack of resources available to document it. It is only through documentation that the usefulness of Dene TEK can become apparent and an improved understanding can be gained of the practices and conditions which lead to the breakdown and also to the re-establishment of Dene management systems. If Dene

TEK is to be revitalised, research must continue to be initiated by the Dene themselves, under the guidance of the elders and with the cooperation of the youth.

Reconciling two profoundly different world views is no simple task. The spiritually based ethic that governs the interaction between the Dene spiritual, human and natural worlds lies in direct contrast to the Western scientific explanation of environmental phenomena which is based on the setting up and testing of hypotheses and the establishment of theories and general laws. However, spiritual explanations often conceal practical conservation strategies and can aid the making of appropriate decisions about the wise use of resources. The Dene system exists within an entirely different cultural experience and set of values, one which paints no more and no less valid a picture of reality.

Just as the scientific establishment is often reluctant to accept the validity of Dene TEK because of the spiritual element, so the Dene are sometimes hesitant to accept Western science because of what appears to be its overriding need to control and interfere with nature. Environmental scientists are viewed as constantly tagging and capturing animals and digging holes in the ground. While there can be no denying the socially and ecologically destructive impact Western science and technology may have had on Dene culture, in some instances it may be able to provide information that is otherwise unavailable, for example, a view of ecological phenomena at the microscopic level or over large distances.

To remedy such mutual suspicions and misunderstandings, local people must become directly involved in the research, not least because this "inside" perspective is essential if the information is to be integrated accurately. Moreover, it is a fundamental right of the Dene, or any local people for that matter, to have control over research that directly affects them. As a part of this collaborative arrangement, training programmes which include hands-on learning experience must be made available to both groups. All too often it is the indigenous researcher who is taught the scientific method and forced to adapt his or her cultural reality to that model.

While it is essential that TEK research involve people who possess an appropriate background in biology, ecology and resource management, it is also essential to include people with social science skills. TEK cannot be properly understood if it is analysed independently of the social and political structure in which it is embedded. The social perspective includes the way people perceive, use, allocate, transfer and manage their natural resources. Dene TEK is rooted in an oral tradition and concerned primarily with qualitative observations. Gathering both biological data and information about the local social-political structure can best be accomplished through talking with people and participating directly in harvesting activities. Social scientists bring these skills to TEK research along with their ability to help translate information from one culture to another.

Finally, much of the scepticism towards Dene TEK stems from belief that, while it may have functioned well in the past, it is disappearing with the assimilation of Dene into Euro-Canadian culture, and by the failure of elders to pass on their knowledge to younger generations. While it is undoubtedly true that some erosion of TEK has taken place, informants of the pilot project emphasise that TEK is changing or evolving rather than dying out.

The last problem related to the integration of Dene TEK and Western science is clearly linked to the question of political power. At present, co-management regimes represent the most widespread attempt to integrate TEK and Western science in northern Canada. These vary in their structure and in the degree of power accorded the participating user groups, but most groups have only an advisory capacity. It remains to be seen to what extent these regimes actually incorporate innovative strategies for problem solving, as opposed to using TEK merely to provide data for a decentralised state system which continues to adhere to the Western scientific paradigm, and continues to do the managing. Successful integration of Dene TEK and Western science depends upon the ability of both groups to develop an appreciation of and sensitivity to the respective strengths and limitations of their knowledge systems. In this, oral testimony can play a significant part.

Talking back: the role of oral testimony in participatory development

Nigel Cross

In 1986, at a conference on drought and desertification, satellite images of Africa held international experts spellbound. Two photographic images, taken a year apart, and costing tens of thousands of dollars, showed either the "advancing" Sahara or the "retreating" vegetation in lurid colour. The course of the Nile was particularly clear. A few weeks earlier, at Taragma village, Nile Province, Sudan, an elderly villager was entertaining a small group of visitors from the UK development agency SOS Sahel. Stepping outside his front door he pointed towards nothing—just a wide expanse of desert occasionally relieved by the odd, unpalatable, unburnable shrub. Here, he said, just 40 years ago the trees and shrubs were so numerous that it was difficult to ride a donkey to market without getting scratched.

Satellite imagery and oral testimony both have a part to play in shaping our understanding of environmental change. The people on the ground, several miles below the camera, know exactly what has happened in their locality; they may be amused or interested by the broader picture, but they can't see that it tells them anything they don't already know. They have been taking mental snapshots all their lives.

A few kilometres south of Taragma, an eminent foreign consultant was being given a tour of village tree nurseries by the local manager. The consultant advised the manager that he was growing the wrong species in the wrong place—never mind that they had been successfully propagated, planted and protected for the last 20 years. The manager's opinion was not solicited.

The problem facing those who give weight to indigenous knowledge is that they come face to face with the weight, indeed might, of the multilateral and bilateral aid business with its armies of highly qualified agronomists and economists, with its satellites, laboratories and computers. Oral testimony is regarded as anecdotal, even endearing, but not very reliable. Its fringe appeal is the greatest enemy of its credibility. Yet it seemed obvious to SOS Sahel that oral history methods, applied to development projects, would create important space for the hitherto silenced majority to speak out about their concerns and priorities directly, rather than through the medium of a team of consultants, or local officials with vested interest.

In 1987 SOS Sahel was approached by HelpAge International for ideas to support the elderly in the Sahelian zone, and was able to put its theory into practice. SOS Sahel finances environment projects which aim to increase food production through sustainable investment in natural resource management. Such long-term work offers few obvious benefits to the elderly. But project informants, like the old man at Taragma, had been an enormous help both in advising project staff and in encouraging younger, stronger, people to invest time and labour in shelterbelt planting and soil and water conservation.

While it was unclear how SOS Sahel could help the elderly, it was strikingly clear that the elderly could be actively involved in development work. The idea for an oral history project which would systematically record traditional environmental knowledge (TEK) and chronicle environmental change took shape. By talking at length with elderly farmers, pastoralists, refugees and other groups in the Sahel, the project hoped to gain a better understanding of traditional land-use practice, land tenure, farming and pastoral systems, the causes of desertification and many other aspects of Sahelian life. The aim was not only to record TEK and improve rapport with the people with whom SOS Sahel and its partner agencies work, but also to develop a practical methodology which could be incorporated into development planning, implementation and evaluation.

Thus the Sahel Oral History Project (SOHP) was motivated by twin concerns: to complement or if necessary correct, the "expertise" of donor agencies by focusing on indigenous knowledge; and to value and learn from those people who had lived through unprecedented social and environmental change and who were, for the most part, illiterate, "uneducated" experts in their own lives.

From the beginning, this was not a grassroots-inspired project, although it worked at village level. No community had asked for it, and it was initiated and designed from the outside. To complement the powerful satellite images the project chose to work across the Sahelian zone—a continent-wide area of low rainfall and poor soils. Sites were selected because they were areas of continuing project work for SOS Sahel and sister agencies, although efforts were made to work in non-project areas as a comparison.

Because SOHP had limited resources, few national-level research organisations could be involved; their tenders were simply too expensive. Project partners were largely existing development projects who provided logistical support, and whose staff acted as interviewers. While this led to effective collaboration at the agency and community level, it also served to reinforce SOHP as an exercise in North-South dialogue rather than involving or encouraging a wider discussion at the national or pan-Sahelian level. So while SOHP solicited the individual experience and the individual or community-level agenda, it did not engage in a wider consultative process (although the published transcripts have since made a contribution). With just £60,000 (US$90,000) to spend in eight countries it opted for something less than perfect, and less than fully participatory.

The collection process

Preliminary research, identification of sites, liaison with other agencies and the development of a questionnaire and guidelines were carried out by SOS Sahel in London. But while the coordination team were European, the interviewers themselves were all local to the interview areas or fluent in the local language. Whether project workers, students or journalists, the most successful interviewers were good listeners who had a natural curiosity and interest in the respondents. As interviewers also had to translate and transcribe the recorded interviews into French or English, a relatively high level of education was required. While it proved difficult to employ educated women, in the end all the interviews with women were by women [1].

The time allocated to the actual interviews in each country was about one month. A three-day training programme preceded the interviews, involving a review of the questionnaire, role-play and a "pilot" interview and transcription. From the beginning, it was stressed that the questionnaire was intended to be flexible. It was adapted to the particular experience of the respondent—pastoralist, farmer, man, woman—as required. There were sections on family history, occupation, descriptions of the changing environment, vegetation, farming and livestock practices, and the impact of development as well as of drought.

Each interviewer was given the opportunity to revise questions in the light of specific cultural and socio-economic factors. In effect, the questionnaire was a checklist of themes to be discussed, rather than a punishing question-by-question ordeal. While this helped to create a more natural conversational environment, it inevitably affected the detail and organisation of the interview. Opportunities for follow-up questions which would have led to greater definition were sometimes missed. Rigour was sacrificed, in some instances, to ramble.

Thus, what had set out to be an indigenous knowledge collection project became much more a vehicle for individual views and priorities to surface. The Western scientific concern to establish the facts, to collect, enumerate and name the parts, gave way to a more political, even poetical exercise where individual perceptions were accorded status and value, regardless of whether they were lucid and apparently correct, or inconsistent and contradictory.

By the end of 1990, over 500 interviews amounting to about 600 hours of tapes had been completed, of which a little less than half were with women. The project worked in Senegal, Mauritania, Burkina Faso, Chad, Sudan and Ethiopia—at 19 different sites in 17 different languages. Despite the level of variable detail, the interviews describe a wide range of environmental knowledge and traditional farming and pastoral systems. Farmers talk about tried and tested methods of improving soil fertility; pastoralists explain how they control animal reproduction, the pastures preferred by each of their animals and the ideal ratio of males to females. The practices and remedies of traditional midwives are mentioned, as are the skills of blacksmiths, *marabouts* and *griots*.

Change is everywhere recorded. There is clear agreement about the reasons for environmental degradation and the part humans and animals have played in it: lower rainfall, inappropriate development, and population growth leading to pressure on marginal areas, in turn squeezing pastoralism on to smaller and smaller grazing lands. Bush is being cleared to make new land available for (short-term) commercial and subsistence farming. The increased pressure on land and natural resources has disrupted what was "previously an amicable relationship between farmers and pastoralists [2]".

An agricultural botanist with a wide knowledge of the agro-ecological zone reviewed the interviews. He reported that "SOHP has highlighted the changes that have taken place in the Sahel within living memory", but he found it difficult to quantify these changes—although one major difference is that farmers now cultivate three to five times as much land as 30 years ago, "in the uncertain hope of a subsistence yield". Given that the "extra" land cultivated is either very marginal or was formerly communal grazing land, the prospects for sustainable farming are considered to be fairly dire. Although there has been a lack of organised statistical evidence, much ecological information collection by the SOHP is still being analysed, and a botanical glossary based on the collection has filled in some gaps in the standard reference works.

Perceptions of environmental change are embedded in a social and cultural context. The SOHP established a fuller picture of community history and social evolution than originally anticipated. The interviews reveal the impact of increased migration and are particularly vivid on the extent of the breakdown of traditional relationships between groups: adults and children; farmers, pastoralists and agro-pastoralists; men and women; even man and beast. Much of the information contradicts received development wisdom and provides ample evidence, if evidence were needed, that many conference generalisations simply do not stand up (particularly in the area of gender and labour) or are so general as to be seriously misleading [3].

Above all each interview has the potential to illuminate life in the Sahel, not only for foreign aid workers, but also for the extensive class of educated public servants who every day take critical decisions on behalf of their "unschooled", distantly related fellow citizens. "My father", says the Minister, "was a peasant farmer." But the interviews show how quickly traditional knowledge has been rejected by the son.

Returning the evidence

Many oral history projects get stuck after the collection phase. What to do with those boxes of tapes, those untidy transcripts—how to interpret them? How to publish them? How to return them to the informants? All these questions were considered by the SOHP at the beginning of the project, and several years later the answers are still evolving.

The first, and perhaps most critical stage is the return, somehow, of the interviews to their owners. Once translated and transcribed, however, they are beyond the reach of the community which prepared them. Perhaps because the SOHP was conceived by outsiders there was no clamour for the establishment of local oral history collections. However, the process of collection was in itself perhaps the single most valuable contribution the project was able to make to both individuals and participating communities.

It became clear that one of the immediate and significant benefits of SOHP was that it literally forced participating agencies to create the time to listen; with the result that project workers, even those born and raised in the community, achieved a new understanding of, and respect for, traditional knowledge. The coordinator of SOHP in Mali noted that the quality of individual knowledge and experience came as a surprise to the interviewers—project workers with more than a touch of superiority about their own educational achievements:

> *The interviews helped to counteract the idea that farmers are ignorant, conservative and fatalistic. Such preoccupations persist among project staff but they are more subliminal than explicit...the more details we have of farmers' knowledge and ingenuity, the more we can hope to counteract these problems of attitude.*

The interviewers themselves discovered how little they knew of their own culture and of their parents' generation. Familiar objects took on new meaning, for instance: "I did not know that in the past, the kitchen hearth is always facing west...I asked why. They told me the dead are buried...facing east. The wind, which comes from the west, carries smoke with it. This way, the smoke won't get in a person's eyes. We really believe in this, because for us the dead are not really dead." A small thing perhaps, but "the research allowed me to trace my roots, to discover where I really came from".

One project associated with the SOHP has managed to return the interviews directly. The Fédération des Paysans Organisés du Département de Bakel, in Senegal, has developed a literacy programme using the oral history interviews.

> We wanted to participate [in the SOHP] from the start because we realised that it would be of benefit to our own work— particularly to our literacy trainers. What might have seemed like a lot of extra work in fact worked out to our advantage. We put our trust in young inexperienced workers and were delighted to discover they were able to carry out the work well...in addition they discovered a rich well of knowledge.

Transforming the spoken into the written word, however, does demand a certain amount of editorial judgement if it is to be more than simply a tool for literacy. But there is great potential for literacy work, and for developing local education materials from oral testimony. In most instances however, the SOHP did not transcribe the tapes into the local language. This was partly because of the time factor, and partly because a few of the 17 languages concerned were essentially oral languages without an agreed and standardised written alphabet. But it was mainly because the major benefit of transcripts to a non-literate community is in literacy training or in helping to conserve a language under threat—and these were not, at the time, project priorities. However, requests for the return of the tapes for literacy programmes have since been received from some participating projects. In general, however, it is probably best to design an oral history project for literacy purposes around less specific themes.

For the informants themselves, there were at least some chances to influence the course of development in the area. But the immediate benefit for those interviewed was that, at last, someone was paying respectful attention, not just at an official meeting orchestrated by the project manager and the village chief, but to individuals with their own strongly held opinions based on their own unique experiences. The elderly were especially glad to discover that their knowledge was valued and appreciated by the "educated" young.

It is, then, difficult to point to a single consequence—such as a new well, the re-adoption of a half-forgotten irrigation technique, the testing of indigenous remedies—that followed from the interviews, although undoubtedly some projects have acted on this new body of information. Rather, it is possible to point to a more sympathetic atmosphere, and a greater understanding of the elusive concept of participation.

Each development project associated with SOHP was at a different stage. In Mali, oral history was used as part of the wider "getting-to-know-you" phase at the beginning of the project. In Niger, oral testimony was collected at the pre-planning phase, and the woman interviewer was subsequently employed by the project as a senior extension worker. In Sudan, it became clear that oral testimony could be a powerful evaluation tool. A comment in an interview with a woman in an SOS Sahel project area—"I am suspicious of their activities. They will probably take our land and we may never see it again"—underlined the need to improve the extension activities. The project's education unit designed a *marud*, a travelling exhibition including photos, maps and three-dimensional models to tour the villages. Isolated comments do not as a rule prove anything one way or another, and are indeed "anecdotal" when published out of context. But in the context of a development activity, where the project workers and local services are witness to the individual testimony, the testimony empowers the individual.

Publication and dissemination

The publication of the interviews took several forms designed to reach a variety of audiences. The first stage was what might be called "Samizdat" publishing; the production of typed English transcripts, including translations from Francophone Africa. These were publicised at workshops, seminars and through the Sahelian and dryland networks, while the preparation of a paperback selection was in progress.

The usefulness of the collection in this typed form was dramatically enhanced by the production of an index. The index was itself a selection; to have included every reference to a theme would, in some cases, have led to 500 entries. Instead it highlighted those entries which, in the judgement of the indexers, constituted the most important or interesting examples. Without an index (as distinct from a catalogue of interviews) such a collection gathers dust. In contrast, by using the SOHP index, the editor of *Grasshoppers and Locusts: The plague of the Sahel*, for example, was able to check references to the pests throughout the Sahel—including traditional methods of locust control [4]. Other writers and editors have used the collection in similar fashion, as have newspapers, magazines and professional journals seeking "authentic" material.

Although an index makes a collection accessible, it also facilitates a "rent-a-quote" approach. On more than one occasion SOHP found that selective quotation had been used either to bolster a fundraising proposal or to lend credibility to a contentious argument. There is no effective copyright in oral testimony, and indeed, if the purpose is to add vibrant, first-hand experience to inform a serious debate, little would be achieved by sealing such testimony in a copyright box. On numerous occasions interviewees expressed the hope that their stories would receive the widest possible dissemination. And perhaps dissemination is the best defence against appropriation—for the more people who are familiar with the material, the harder it becomes to misappropriate it.

All those involved in the project recognised from the outset the potential for oral testimony to counteract the media coverage of drought and famine and the "victim" stereotype so often reinforced by the fundraising publicity of aid agencies. Some 80 interviews, both representative and of intrinsic narrative interest, were selected for *At The Desert's Edge: Oral histories from the Sahel*, which has now been published in English (1991), Dutch (1992), and French (1993) [5].

As well as providing the first Sahelian-authored account of the realities of life in the Sahel for a European audience—schools, colleges, unions, churches, clubs and charity supporters—*At The Desert's Edge* was also aimed at decision makers. The hope was that development planners and area specialists might manage a little bedtime reading from a text that would confront them with real people with real names, as opposed to a lumpen class of "beneficiaries" who inhabit policy reports and technical papers, and nowhere else.

To some extent this aspiration materialised—though largely as a consequence of free distribution of the book to policy makers. For instance, the Director of the World Bank's Sahelian department read the book and visited London, to discuss the relevance of oral history to the Bank's programme. This discussion has been both tantalising and inconclusive: attempts to mesh the very specific and very particular (oral testimony) into the very large and very general (Bank policy) is far from easy. Although it is engaged in "beneficiary assessment" exercises, the Bank is working to a timetable which makes it difficult to take oral testimony on board. Like others who have embraced Participatory Rural Appraisal (PRA) as a simple formula for ensuring people's participation in development projects, the Bank is attracted to "rapid" survey techniques without always recognising that PRA evolved from Rapid Rural Appraisal (RRA)—junking "rapid" in favour of "participatory". Meaningful participation is not possible on flying visits. Oral testimony takes time, and requires a longer-term investment than most monitoring and evaluation departments are prepared or equipped for.

The final phase of publication has been the organisation of all the interviews, in English, by country, on computer disk, together with a computerised and hard copy index. As this has taken two years of largely volunteer labour, there are inevitable inaccuracies and imperfections. But it is now possible to receive all 500 interviews, or country-by-country interviews, on disk. Disk publishing—like microfilm publishing before it—is the logical way to ensure that a major resource (amounting to 800,000 words) reaches an interested, engaged and expert audience of academics, researchers and development consultants. It is also, of course, a means of conserving an important resource on recent Sahelian environmental history.

Application

At an early stage after the indexing, and after the two project directors had read all the transcripts, SOS Sahel held an in-house seminar to consider the main themes arising from the project which might inform its own development planning. Two themes in particular seemed to require further research: an analysis of the level and types of participation by the "beneficiaries" in planning, monitoring and evaluation; and the consequences of male out-migration on women and their household and environmental management.

The Participatory Evaluation Project (PEP) was conceived as a response to the numerous instances where interviewees described the totalitarian nature of so much development. The heart of the project was an appraisal of techniques such as PRA, and development theatre, as well as oral testimony itself, in an attempt to identify what constitute successful participatory mechanisms in development projects [6].

The migration research began as a more academic exercise, although it hoped to identify "action points" that would help development projects become more responsive to the consequences of male out-migration, and to the needs of migrants' wives and families. The research employed classic social science approaches—use of the questionnaire survey, sample-frames, focus group discussions, data-processing and statistical analysis. The aim was to produce convincing and detailed data, that would to some extent support and illuminate the voices of the women interviewed in the SOHP.

At about the same time another SOS Sahel research project on food security issues and employment "safety-nets" was taking place in Ethiopia, using similar social science methodologies. Some 600 questionnaire interviews were conducted by six local researchers in Koisha, Ethiopia, as the research component of an SOS Sahel cash-for-work road-building programme. Again the data was carefully processed, and a fascinating if confusing picture emerged of the relevant benefits and disadvantages of "cash-for-work" over "food-for-work", of the profile of those who opted in to the project, and of their varying preferences according to age, gender and occupation.

On reviewing the quantitative results of both the migrant research project and the Food Security Project (FSP), it became clear that there were still larger questions, indeed new larger questions, thrown up by the surveys that needed further investigation. It was decided to return to oral testimony collection as a way not only of pursuing the ambiguous and paradoxical, but also of making the thicket of facts and figures meaningful—alive. The assumption that orthodox, donor-approved social science methods would illuminate the oral history had, once again, to be turned on its head.

A different kind of questionnaire, thematic rather than quantitative, was developed with the help of the local FSP researchers. The questionnaire was a framework within which the 40 or 50 interviewees would be free to set their own priorities as well as shed more light on specific issues which interested the project, such as common grazing rights and people's wider perceptions of land use. Despite role play and practice interviews the oral testimony collection proved more difficult than anticipated. Transcription was a problem, for although the interviews were conducted in the local language, its complex orthography necessitated translation into the more familiar Amharic (see p88).

But the major obstacle was the researchers' own bias: they had just spent three months as enumerators, checking off a list of pre-set questions. They found it both difficult and exhausting to switch gear into the more free-flowing, attentive, listening mode required by the oral historian. They and the national research director complained that the respondents wouldn't stop talking, that they rambled. "I think", he wrote, "that we should exert more influence on the sequencing of the topics for discussion to avoid redundancy and keep the interest of the interviewee up to the end." Adjustments were made and the interviewing continued.

Despite the fears and worries of the collectors the final product has indeed illuminated the research (one interview was 42 pages long). The "rambles", although sometimes inconsequential, are as often packed with clues and insights. For example, although it was not the intention of the interviews to seek opinion, let alone evaluation, of a neighbouring water-provision and primary health care project, the frequency of comment on it amply demonstrates its impact in the area and has provided the agency involved with useful, unsolicited feedback. Also the interviews gave rich detail about community and family support structures, which the formal questionnaire had been unable to elicit.

This is not to jettison quantitative methods, which provide thought-provoking base-line data, but to illustrate that individual responses, prejudices and interpretation can help make sense of it all. Inevitably oral testimony also throws up other questions, other conundrums. The research director of the FSP is both delighted and infuriated by the new oral testimonies, leading to new questions and answers, and new puzzles and potential solutions.

SOS Sahel has learnt that its oral testimony practice does not need to be confined to a discrete oral history project, such as the SOHP, but continues to burst into life in unexpected places. In Wollo, Ethiopia, an extended PRA exercise as part of a project planning phase had failed to report the existence of a significant Muslim minority in the middle of an area famed for its orthodox church. A mini oral testimony project is now focusing on the influence of religion and traditional custom in Wollo, an area which has more saints' days (holidays) that impinge on working practices than the Vatican City.

Oral testimony, insofar as it has application to development projects, is as much a process as it is a product. It informs, illuminates and above all recognises the identity of someone who might otherwise remain an anonymous "beneficiary". It is a new and extensive training resource, it is an expressive and potent medium for development education, it is a supplementary feeding programme for skeletal data. And perhaps most important of all, it amplifies the voices of the non-literate, non-participants in the United Nation's fifth development decade.

CHAPTER SIX

IN THEIR OWN WORDS
The strengths and weaknesses of oral testimony

He's convinced that we are attacking them, doing violence to their culture...that with our tape recorders and our ball-point pens we are the worm that works its way in the fruit and rots it.
Mario Vargas Llosa, The Storyteller

Eyewitnesses of the same occurrence gave different accounts of them as they remembered or were interested in the actions of one side or another.
Thucydides, History of the Peloponesian Wars, 420 BC

For as long as people have been listening to each other, they have been aware of the need to treat what they hear with caution. As Thucydides and Vargas Llosa imply, there are some hard questions to be asked about the credibility of oral testimony, and the ethics of its collection and application. In this chapter, we look at some of the special problems associated with oral evidence, most notably the potential misuse, misappropriation or exploitation of people's words and knowledge, and the ambiguities and difficulties inherent in evaluating and interpreting individual testimony.

Implicit in any critical and responsible use of oral testimony is the recognition that any listening is, in part, a transaction of some kind, and that its interpretation is not a simple process. Awareness of the complexities and responsibilities involved should help practitioners to draw the most out of people's testimony without distorting its meaning or abusing their confidence. The more practical and interpretational issues to consider are: the nature of memory; the value of opinion; the place of myth, legend and proverb; the impact of the interviewer; the implications of transferring testimony to secondary formats; and the extent to which individual testimony can be regarded as representative. The main ethical issues concern the potential intrusion into people's lives, and their right of ownership over what they say, and over how their testimony is presented and disseminated.

Interpreting oral testimony

The nature of memory

Memory is the raw material of much oral testimony and it is therefore important to have some understanding of how memory works and the kind of information it produces. Far from being a computer-like act of "automatic recall", memory is a creative process. All memory, whether short- or long-term, is stored through a process of selection and interpretation. This sifting and shaping is most acute immediately after an event, but, more slowly and subtly, it continues in the long term too. The process of ordering, discarding, selecting and combining means that memory is always a combination of the objective and subjective, and of facts, interpretation and opinion [1].

The depth and detail of individual memory also varies, reflecting personal interest and experience. Self-justification and catharsis can influence what is remembered; fear or trauma can lead to conscious or unconscious repression. "Forget that story; if we tell it our lineage will be destroyed," exclaimed a Tanzanian with a family tradition of conflict with the ruling dynasty, quoted in Steven Feierman's *The Shambaa Kingdom* [2]. Equally, certain well-rehearsed "set pieces" and anecdotes will assume a special importance, perhaps beyond their original significance, because they have proved to be so popular and gripping as stories.

Memory sometimes "telescopes" events, making sense of the past by combining into one event the details of several separate episodes. How people foresee the future can also influence their presentation of the past. We may adapt what we remember so that it reflects subsequent events more accurately, thus presenting ourselves and our judgements in a better light.

Loops and strands

When interviewing older people, researchers should bear in mind the additional effects age has on memory. On the one hand, old age can revitalise long-term memory through the process of "life review", which often follows retirement or bereavement, when people reflect on their whole lives and typically feel a wish to convey their memories to others before they die. This process often brings back especially vivid memories of earlier years, usually much clearer than those of yesterday or last week. In later old age, on the other hand, a person's memory may become less agile, less able to jump from one theme to another. Particular lines of thought may have to be followed through as if in "loops", working through each cycle of memory until the narrator comes full circle and can then start on another subject. The resulting oral testimonies are therefore often made up of strands of memory born out of particular mental associations, rather than a historical sequence of events.

Memory, whatever one's age, is thus a continuing process of editing and selection, often influenced by hindsight. These characteristics mean that we should never assume the information produced from memory to be unadulterated fact. Memory does contain facts, but as they are remembered—which may not be exactly as they happened. In this sense, memory is more a creative than a mechanical act. It intertwines the biographical bones of a particular life with clues to the narrator's ideas and consciousness, what they judge to be important, how they have interpreted and come to terms with their experience, and how they relate to others. Learning how, in any given culture, to distinguish these different strands in memory is fundamental to the interpretation of oral testimony, especially life histories. When oral testimony can be set against other evidence, or one testimony can be compared with another, the variations in accounts, which might be thought a weakness, can be turned into a special strength, an insight into how people make sense of their lives and social worlds. Indeed, it is the very mixture of the subjective and the objective which makes oral testimony such a rich source of information, revealing as much about values and perceptions as about material realities.

Overleaf is a description of the way in which a Peruvian development organisation used social science methods to analyse testimonies and draw out information in order to improve services for women struggling to survive in the poor districts of Lima. As Peruvian social scientist Sara Pait

Interpreting testimony: a multi-disciplinary approach

Collecting oral testimonies is a challenging process; interpreting them is another, in many ways more complex, task. How do organisations draw information and insights from the rich personal material of life stories which will be of benefit to the wider community's development?

A project in Lima, Peru, has been exploring different approaches to interpreting oral testimonies. INPET (Instituto Peruano de Promoción del Desarrollo Solidario) is a Lima-based NGO seeking to improve the quality of life for the city's poor communities, especially in the fields of employment and enterprise development. They work with cooperatives, small businesses, grassroots organisations, public service authorities and the self-employed. Their work ranges from running gender awareness campaigns to providing training, credit, technical and marketing advice to small enterprises.

Over a period of several months in 1990, they collected life stories from a group of women with whom they had come into contact during their work. Most were up against obstacles common to those who are poor and female: minimal access to education or training, limited employment opportunities, sexual harassment by colleagues and employers, and the responsibility for bringing up children, often single-handedly. Each story is unique, reflecting the women's personal strengths and weaknesses and those of the people they grew up with or encountered in their struggle to make a life for themselves and their children. Yet while individual circumstances vary, and reactions to events differ, analysis also reveals common threads and influences.

INPET subjected the testimonies to analysis in several different disciplines in order to draw out information about the kind of institutions (family, state, neighbourhood, religious, charitable and private enterprise) and services (health, education, credit, training, legal, welfare) which have helped or hindered the women. The aim was to identify the women's real needs, to see how far these are being met by the existing community structures and services, and to establish possible improvements to policies. The testimonies were examined, not only by development theorists and practitioners, but by social scientists and other professionals. Both psychoanalysis and Marxist theory were used as tools, in an attempt to distinguish between the truly personal—aspects of an individual's upbringing, for example—and wider social conditioning. "Out of the specific and personal it is possible to learn much about the society which formed the individual," writes Sara Pait, author of *Propiedad, Participación y Solidaridad*, a book about the project [14].

The interviews took place during the second half of 1990, when structural adjustment policies were beginning to bite. They revealed that the resulting loss of some communal kitchens and childcare centres directly and adversely affected the women and their already limited choice of employment. They also showed how hard it was for the women not just practically, but psychologically, to challenge their accepted roles.

Emma, who ended up being a driving force behind her community's cooperatives and women's committees, became an activist almost by default. She took on the role of neighbourhood coordinator after receiving threats that electricity and water supplies would be cut off. As her confidence and abilities developed, she faced opposition from her husband as well as gossip and backbiting from neighbours. She had no desire to challenge the status quo but saw her community work as stemming from a desire, since childhood, to help others, and as reflecting her innate ability to organise, severely tested under the strain of holding together a large and impoverished extended family. It is almost as though she views it as her fate, rather than any conscious direction she has taken: "The enthusiasm to help others took me....I was born with that.....[if I can't do that] I'll feel uncomfortable, bundled." When INPET got social scientists to study a testimony such as Emma's, one of the strands they tried to unravel was the complicated relationship between different social groups. Many different factors cause people to oppose or to ally with one another: gender, culture, ethnicity, economic interests, occupation or beliefs. More understanding of the way these forces interact in any community will help development initiatives.

Victoria, who ended up running a small carpentry workshop with another woman, found herself breaking the conventional mould out of a combination of economic imperatives and chance. Her testimony reveals much about the kind of practical and moral support, and training, she and her partner needed, but often lacked, in building up their business. Her story contains information about the special needs of women, particularly single parents, if they are to cope with all the different responsibilities and challenges of taking on "men's work", being self-employed and managing a business which involves both creating and marketing goods.

From just two testimonies details emerge not only about women's practical concerns, but also their wider needs as mothers, producers and community members. By showing how social and personal forces interact, INPET hopes to persuade and help social scientists, planners and development workers to listen with more attention to personal needs and priorities for what these reveal about the realities of the wider community.

explained, by comparing the different testimonies and using other sources of information, the researchers aimed to unravel "the social factors which influence an entire generation" and "the individual factors which confer someone's unique personal characteristics [3]".

Opinion

The great strength of oral testimony is its ability to capture personal experience and individual perception. Oral testimony thus produces "opinionated" material in the best sense of the word. However, it needs to be recognised as such. One person's testimony represents one particular perspective and not an overview. Much "information" is likely to be within the realms of conviction and belief rather than undisputed evidence, and many apparently factual statements will in reality represent people's judgement on an issue. People's judgements and opinions are, of course, open to debate and alternative viewpoints on many issues exist within and outside any community. Some opinions have been deeply considered and are based on extensive knowledge; others may be more in the nature of hunches, intuition or simple prejudice. They all reveal something about individual and collective values.

The element of subjective opinion in individual testimonies should always be recognised. If not, there is the risk that the general is extrapolated from the particular when this is inappropriate. For example, men's opinions of farming in a community might be heard as representing the experience of women farmers too, yet the social and economic context within which women farm is likely to be significantly different. Similarly, different groups in a community may not share the

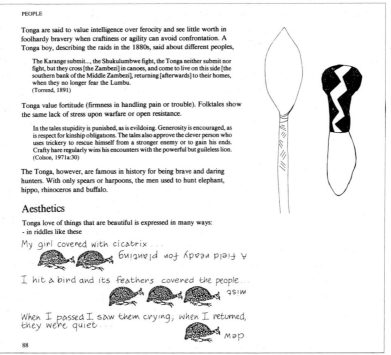

PEOPLE

Tonga are said to value intelligence over ferocity and see little worth in foolhardy bravery when craftiness or agility can avoid confrontation. A Tonga boy, describing the raids in the 1880s, said about different peoples,

> The Karange submit..., the Shukulumbwe fight, the Tonga neither submit nor fight, but they cross [the Zambezi] in canoes, and come to live on this side [the southern bank of the Middle Zambezi], returning [afterwards] to their homes, when they no longer fear the Lumbu.
> (Torrend, 1891)

Tonga value fortitude (firmness in handling pain or trouble). Folktales show the same lack of stress upon warfare or open resistance.

> In the tales stupidity is punished, as is evildoing. Generosity is encouraged, as is respect for kinship obligations. The tales also approve the clever person who uses trickery to rescue himself from a stronger enemy or to gain his ends. Crafty hare regularly wins his encounters with the powerful but guileless lion.
> (Colson, 1971a:30)

The Tonga, however, are famous in history for being brave and daring hunters. With only spears or harpoons, the men used to hunt elephant, hippo, rhinoceros and buffalo.

Aesthetics

Tonga love of things that are beautiful is expressed in many ways:
- in riddles like these

My girl covered with cicatrix . . .   A field ready for planting

I hit a bird and its feathers covered the people . . .   mist

When I passed I saw them crying; when I returned, they were quiet . . .   Map

88

A page from **Lwaano Lwanyika,** *a book about and produced with the Tonga people of the Zambezi Valley. Containing stories, interviews, poems and a wealth of detail on their culture and resources, the book highlights the importance of proverbs and riddles as a means of expression for the Tonga [15].*

same sense of "progress": for some, any money saved is best spent on education; for others, investing in livestock or building a house which can be handed down for generations is their main priority.

Thus one of the great values of collecting testimony is that it highlights the diversity of human experience, values and aspirations. There is no doubt that it is possible to construct reliable information from a group of interviews of, for example, changes in agricultural, forestry or fishing practices, in gender roles or patterns of migration, marriage or childrearing. On the other hand, people will give different accounts of the reasons for change and of the impacts. What these accounts reveal is how change was experienced and remembered. Equally, many of the versions of events or stories that people tell are not factually exact or literally true. Yet these "untrue" stories, just because they show more clearly how people make sense of their lives through combining and re-ordering memories, and sometimes even adding touches to them, can often be the clearest indicators of their consciousness, their ways of thinking and sense of self. Similarly, the way broader social units—the family, the community, national or ethnic groups—relate to collective memory and myth can reveal much, not only about their past, but also about how they see and shape their present and future.

Myth, legend and proverb

Oral testimony is not only personally subjective, based on memory and opinion, but culturally subjective, drawing on collective myth and legend. In the introduction to her book, *The Story of an African Famine*, Megan Vaughan asks the kind of question which has to be faced by most people who are working with oral testimony. Speaking about the different kinds of evidence she gathered, she asked: "What weight, for instance, should one give to the information that the goats sold by famine victims changed into snakes when taken home by their new owners [4]?"

As Vaughan has noted, this kind of symbolic material can be "difficult to accommodate" and hard to interpret. Yet a commitment to listening means coming to terms with forms of thought and expression used in different cultures. Many traditional cultures still place great importance on speaking figuratively and people's speech is frequently laced with magical stories, legends and proverbs. Interviewers may find their questions answered by a further cryptic question and a knowing look, or their enquiries met with an enigmatic proverb. Some of these will be more immediately obvious in their meaning than others.

As the case study on the Dene's traditional environmental knowledge makes clear (see p116), not all knowledge systems are as empirically driven as Western systems, which tend to operate on the basis that there are logical answers to most questions. Many cultures are quite comfortable with the concept that some types of question are unanswerable: the power of mystery, the validity of myth, the superiority of God's knowledge, and the simple fact of not knowing are perfectly acceptable [5]. The wise person in such cultures may be regarded as the one who knows how best to re-phrase a question rather than how to answer it in the strict sense. He or she may meet one mystery with another, or a question with a riddle. This more oblique form of response is often given through mythical stories or proverbs.

Megan Vaughan's question about what weight should be given to such stories is critical. Where a significant part of people's testimony is couched in figurative language, much of it initially obscure to the outsider, there may be a temptation to ignore some of the material and discard it as untranslatable or even irrelevant. However, making the effort to unpack the meaning of stories and sayings is crucial and can often yield valuable insights. When listening to an account of goats turning into snakes, the natural tendency of the literal-minded Westerner is to "de-mythologise", but there is likely to be an important message in the myth. The transformation of a goat, bought from a famine victim, into a snake is a powerful image which may have been evoked in order to condemn the transaction. It would then be worth investigating why such a transaction is viewed as bad. There may be complex economic reasons, or the image may reflect more simple moral or cultural strictures. On the other hand, the story could simply be an exaggerated way of epitomising the terrible supernatural chaos and confusion of the famine days when all coping strategies seemed cursed, all relations soured, and when there was no way out for anyone—even those with money. Either way, it is worth preserving such a story and persevering with its interpretation to find one or many meanings.

The same problems arise with the use of proverbs and riddles, which can seem cryptic in the extreme. Sahelian proverbs are as numerous as they are obscure to the outsider, as local interviewers for the Sahel Oral History Project discovered when one of their questions received the one-line response: "The termites are far from the moon [6]"! Yet the obligation to unpack the meaning of these figures of speech remains and can be richly rewarding, for the very brevity of proverbs means they are a particularly sharp expression of a common belief or attitude. Often, exploring the meaning can act as a catalyst for further discussion of these attitudes.

The impact of the interviewer

So far this chapter has focused on the subjectivity of the narrator. However, the collection of oral testimony is usually born out of dialogue, and is the result of an encounter between two or more people—the narrator(s) and the interviewer(s). The latter, and the interview format itself, can influence the shape and content of the material collected.

An interview is never a simple and objective recounting of experience but, rather, a creative discussion governed by particular conditions of time, place and personality. There may be a number of factors which influence the recollection or presentation of experience, over and above the narrator's memory, its detail and selectivity, and his or her skill as a verbal performer. Any audience present will also influence the way narrators shape and emphasise their story, perhaps bending it to what they think the audience wants to hear or sometimes deliberately confusing, confronting or scandalising them. In particular, the skills and motivation of the interviewer will affect the character of the narrator's testimony. The interviewer's special interests, and ability to question and to prompt will determine the interview's flow and direction. The power relationship and degree of rapport between interviewer and narrator will affect its content and tone. The former also brings to the session a particular knowledge base, which is more or less suited to follow up particular leads and avenues in any discussion as it develops.

Equally, the gender dynamics of an interview are bound to have an impact on the testimony, and underline the case for insisting on same-sex interviewers. In some societies, women are unused to or intimidated by talking to outsiders, particularly to men. They may also be unaccustomed to being asked to reflect critically on their situation or to discuss certain aspects of their lives. An interviewer would need to respect and understand this. Moreover, an increasing amount of research into the differences in men's and women's conversational styles shows that (while these obviously vary from culture to culture) in general terms men and women often see a different purpose and opportunity in conversation. For example, whereas men tend to talk about their lives using "I", the active, individual first person, women more often use the collective "we". Socio-linguists believe that for a man, a conversation is likely to be an opportunity to make clear his status and independence in relation to those he is addressing. Women are more likely to see conversation as an opportunity to establish a connection with the other person and may consciously set out to establish rapport. Indeed, a growing number of socio-linguists, such as the American Deborah Tannen, feel that gender differences in conversational style can be so great that every language has a "genderlect", in the same way that it has different dialects [7]. Certainly, interviewers need to distinguish and respect the different conversational styles of men and women in the community in which they are collecting oral testimony.

In the context of relief and development work, it is always desirable to use interviewers who are familiar with or, ideally, originate from the culture of the informants (see p75). However, while an outsider will at least start from the basis that there is much to learn, there is always the danger that "educated" insiders may see themselves as superior to their old community. He or she may be less attentive to the nuances of the interview, or ignore aspects of the narrative which they regard as out of date, unscientific or simply wrong.

As an interviewer, you therefore need to be aware that any oral testimony you collect is "material which you have not just discovered, but in one sense have helped to create [8]". That oral testimony is to some degree co-generated does not undermine the validity of the material produced, but serves to define it more clearly still as a perspective. The very word "interview"—which literally means a "seeing between" or a "view between"—embodies this idea of a particular perspective worked out or created between two parties.

Transfer to secondary formats

The interviewer's influence does not necessarily cease with the end of the interview, because more often than not he or she may then become the translator, editor and possibly even the presenter of the oral testimony material. (The obvious exception is when the narrators themselves edit and present their testimony in community theatre or their own written works.) In all these roles, secondary influence is keenly felt.

Translation and editing inevitably involve tinkering with the original text, and it is these changes and their impact on the meaning of a testimony which make it essential to keep a master tape of the original. This will act as an important point of reference and provide a critical authority for all future interpretations.

Chapter Four looked at some of the difficulties inherent in translation, and described the variety of audio, visual and written forms in which oral testimony can be presented. The great majority of these will involve what a British oral historian, Rebecca Abrams, has regretted as the inevitable "injury" to the original testimony. Writing about her interviews with elderly women, she noted that: "One of the problems of translating an oral history interview into book form is that meaning is injured in the process. Meaning is held not simply in the words, but between the words, in the pauses and hesitations, in the emphasis, inflection, intonation. These things are hard to translate from the spoken voice to the written word [9]." Similar risks are run with the editing and cutting of testimony for audio or visual presentations.

The whole process of moving from the collection of testimony to its presentation for a wider audience inevitably changes the original material to some degree. It is at this point that the issue of context also becomes important. Once it is in a secondary format, a person's testimony can be used in or out of context. The rights and responsibilities this involves are explored under *Dissemination* (see p153).

The question of reliability

Clearly, then, a considerable part of any oral testimony reflects the memory, opinion and culture of the narrator—and, to a lesser extent, the influences of interviewer and editor. These aspects of oral testimony raise important questions about its reliability and its representative nature. Sooner or later, people working with oral testimony come up against the tension between subjective and objective information, and also between qualitative and quantitative data. Part of this tension is created by the bias of the educated and political elite, which tends to exaggerate the objectivity of something which is "down on paper". But this bias aside, there is still a feeling among some professional groups that the information gathered from collecting the spoken word is not as "scientific" as that produced by formal surveys and other "more rigorous" quantitative methods.

When making this distinction, people commonly use the word "anecdotal" to describe, and often to devalue, the kind of material produced as oral testimony. In its strict sense, the word anecdotal means nothing more nor less than "unpublished" (from the greek *anekdota*), but it has nevertheless accrued additional nuances of being unreliable or exaggerated. As the examples in this book have shown, most oral testimony is not anecdotal in the pejorative sense of the word and therefore does not deserve to be dismissed as such. Instead, it needs to be defined more clearly.

Collecting oral testimony is about collecting subjective experience, and it would be wrong to try to compare quantitative and qualitative information as if they were both competitors for the same high ground of objectivity. They are best regarded as complementary—the one informing and qualifying the other. Much of the information which oral testimony produces is, therefore, perhaps best regarded as "insight" rather than data.

On many levels, however, oral testimony can also provide important new factual information. Some of the examples cited earlier show how, in a well-formulated project, people's testimony can reveal much about development issues: the way individuals cope with famine, migration, political struggle or farming technology, for example. But since each account represents a primarily personal viewpoint, it is important not to generalise uncritically from it, or from collections of testimonies. Two basic precautions are needed. First, every project needs, in this respect, to consider very carefully how to select its informants: whether to interview both women and men, different age groups, different social levels, the less articulate as well as the recognised spokepersons.

Second, it must be remembered that the community studied may not be typical. When interesting connections and links are made, or suggestions for further lines of enquiry, these can be explored and tested in other communities. Until then, their relevance should not be assumed. One community's reasons for avoiding immunisation may not be the same as another's, for example, just as one farmer's impression of a farming method may differ from another's, or a woman's experience of social change may not resemble her neighbour's. The testimony of one person or one community can highlight new issues, but only an accumulation of research can show how far it might be representative.

The ethics of oral testimony collection
Intrusion

Because the collection of oral testimony is an intrinsically personal process, it involves important ethical questions. One of the themes of Mario Vargas Llosa's novel, *The Storyteller*, is the potential for destructive cultural intrusion when researchers set about attempting to penetrate, expose, interpret and discuss all aspects of a community's culture [10]. This process can undermine or subtly change a culture by bringing outside influence to bear on custom or belief, which was previously unchallenged and respected. The "tape-recorders" and "ball-point pens" of oral testimony collectors risk being the first part of a process of cultural "rot", although, as the Dene case-study shows, it may also be the last resort of a beleaguered or threatened culture.

Intrusion can also take place at a more individual and personal level. One of oral testimony's particular advantages is its ability to focus on the hidden spheres of life, a person's private world. This can produce a particularly sensitive form of material which needs to be respected if the privacy of the individual or family involved is not to be violated. The process of searching through one's memory can in itself be an emotional and sometimes distressing process. Going back many decades in the space of a two- or three-hour life story interview can shake people up, putting them back in touch with difficult emotions or with a happy past which they may feel is slipping away for ever. Memory may be the raw material of much oral testimony, but the process of recollection may leave narrators feeling raw as well.

There is therefore an important ethical responsibility to respect any difficulty or distress narrators may experience in giving oral testimony. Interviewers should ensure that oral testimony is always collected as sympathetically as possible, with the narrator's right to peace of mind always coming before the interviewer's desire to question. It may be helpful in pre-interview discussions to find out any topics which may be "off limits". Some narrators may not wish to discuss these at all; others may feel the need to speak of them as part of the flow of an interview but will want no record (tape or notes) to be taken while they do so.

The ethical issues to be considered therefore centre around establishing the rights of narrators to privacy and confidentiality, and the extent to which development workers have the right to enquire about and document the knowledge and experience of the people with whom they work. These ethical questions relate to the issue of the extraction and dissemination of knowledge, as well as important concerns about attribution and anonymity.

Ownership and authorship

The issue of rights to privacy and rights over the material generated and collected is often made more difficult by the fact that many poor and/or rural communities lack knowledge about—or access to—any effective copyright or data protection legislation. In the absence of any obvious law on the subject, most ethical relationships between narrators and collectors have to be developed on the basis of trust.

Before agreements can be made about authorship and anonymity, the onus is on the interviewer to explain the purpose of the exercise and to discuss the end-use of the material, and ways of returning the testimony. Most people will be glad to be publicly identified with their testimony, but for others an element of anonymity may be vital. For example, oral testimony has been collected from released child prostitutes in Thailand as part of official reports on this subject. In some cases, children who have given testimony in their own names have subsequently been searched out and contacted time and again by journalists wanting to use their story, causing them much distress and making it almost impossible for them to pick up their lives again. In other situations, understandings about anonymity and attribution are more than legal niceties. In communities where people are living amid conflict, fear or repression, setting such limits can mean the difference between freedom and imprisonment, or even life and death.

In situations where the details of the narrator/interviewer relationship are based on trust rather than defined by law, it is wise to find out what kind of local customs are binding in relation to the protection and respect of a person's word. It might be appropriate to agree to these and to treat them as the equivalent of copyright and protection. Otherwise, it might be best to devise the project's own quasi-legal procedures which protect the narrators and are also easily understood by them.

Dissemination

Similar questions about the rights of ownership come into play when a recorded testimony is transcribed and transferred to secondary formats. Who has the right to determine its form and the extent to which it is disseminated? Who has rights or control over the context in which it is used? Again, the fact that many communities lack access to effective copyright legislation is relevant, and makes it necessary to establish principles of ownership and dissemination on a case-by-case basis.

Chapter One discussed the twofold obligation on the development worker collecting oral testimony: to both "carry forward" and "give back" something of what he or she has heard. Any discussions with people before an oral testimony project should indicate what plans and commitment the interviewer and their organisation have to apply and use what they hear. Methods of dissemination need to be agreed, so that the narrators are aware of the nature of the transaction which will take place when they tell their story or share their experience.

When a community is undertaking its own oral testimony project, this is obviously an obligation which they take upon themselves: to produce a book, perform a play, develop an archive, or lobby for land rights on the basis of their history. In this kind of project, ownership and control over dissemination remain more readily in the hands of those whose words make up the testimony—although, as the Recife case study shows, this can still raise questions within that community (see p112).

In projects involving outsiders, narrators should understand to what extent they are giving their testimony away, and to what extent they will see a return for doing so. This return may be relatively direct like the sharing and exchange of farming techniques through the *Honey Bee* network (see p22), or the opportunity to lobby the government over land rights as in the Solomon Islands (see p50). On the other hand, it may be more for the benefit of others, as in the case of the people of Sudan, Malawi and Mozambique (see pp28-32 and pp34-35) who gave their time and testimony in the hope that the relevant authorities might improve their understanding of famine and displacement and so develop more appropriate responses.

The fact that people's testimony or information may have only an indirect influence on development policy or action can sometimes seem a poor reward for the time and trouble taken. For example, women coping with the aftermath of violence in Sri Lanka were interviewed in order to gain greater understanding of their concerns and priorities, so that agencies might develop more effective ways to mitigate the impacts of conflict [11]. While the women appreciated the object of the exercise, many were also understandably disappointed at the lack of immediate tangible benefits, particularly as some felt they had already answered questions from journalists and aid workers to very little practical effect. This kind of situation does raise awkward questions about the real beneficiaries of such exercises [12]. At the same time, however, many of the women clearly stated that they had benefited from the process of reflection and speaking out, that they appreciated being consulted, and had often gained some new insights into their situations or practical information about sources of assistance. The positive value of simply being listened to—rather than merely questioned—should not be underestimated, as many other projects demonstrate, especially those with the elderly.

Another ethical question concerns the potential misappropriation of testimony. Once an interview has entered the public domain, parts of it can be quoted out of context and it is almost impossible to ensure that it is used only to support appropriate ideas or theories. Nigel Cross, in his case study of the Sahel Oral History Project, points out that in practice it is hard to guard against the "rent-a-quote" approach (see p134). Nevertheless, as far as possible, all users should be made aware of their responsibility to respect the original context in which a testimony was given. While this has obvious legal ramifications in human rights work, the principle is the same whatever the kind of testimony.

Advocacy, fundraising and development education are all activities where there needs to be a respect for testimony and its original meaning. Narrators should be able to assume that, for example, an account told with courage and resourcefulness will not later be presented in a context of dependency or helplessness. The need for NGOs to make an impact and/or to raise money has sometimes led to the use of negative or one-dimensional images. Oral testimony can be used to work against this trend, its strength being that it breaks down stereotypes and represents the voice of individuals, and the complexity of real life.

The challenge

Oral testimony projects tend to produce material which is distinguished by its grasp of the particular, and which recognises many different voices and realities rather than a dominant few. Personal testimony is far more likely to provide an insight or perspective than a comprehensive, objective overview (although these can be written up from a widely researched project). The experience of development agencies so far suggests that oral testimony collection is not a technique which functions best in isolation, but rather benefits from being one of a number of ways of researching and collecting information. The challenge to relief and development workers is therefore to learn how best to interpret and use oral testimony alongside more quantitative methods. As the Italian oral historian Sandro Portelli points out: "The credibility of oral sources is a different credibility....The importance of oral testimony may sometimes lie not in its adherence to facts but rather in its divergence from them, where imagination, symbolism, desire break in [13]." Development which does not reflect people's imagination and desires, and which does not acknowledge and build on local values and knowledge, is unlikely to succeed.

oral testimony work that we have missed and some practical and conceptual considerations which we may have overlooked or not have covered in depth.

As development agencies take more time to listen to people, an increasing amount is being learnt about the methods involved, the subtleties of interpretation, the effectiveness of presentation and the ethics of attribution. It is our hope that this book will start a process which recognises the wealth of experience being gained in oral testimony work around the world, and that this experience will continue to be recorded and exchanged by communities and practitioners through workshops, journals, information networks and, of course, by word of mouth.

Finally, the written word can also make things seem much easier than they actually are in practice. Some of the preceding pages may appear to do this and it may be wise to quote one last piece of oral testimony as a foil to such idealism. At a workshop in Addis Ababa in September 1993, the Ethiopian health educator, Ahmed Mohammed, presented a paper on the use of focus group discussions. In his talk he gave a frank account of the many difficulties involved in bringing people together in such groups and encouraging them to talk. And afterwards, at question time, he uttered a cautionary admonishment to the writers of books such as this one:

> *Those people who designed it [focus group methodology], they must have just sat in their office and wrote it. They do not know about the problems in the field. It is not as easy as it is on paper [1].*

These words apply equally well to all the other methods we have described in the previous chapters. Collecting, interpreting and disseminating oral testimony is certainly not as easy as it may appear on paper. But, despite the practical and conceptual challenges involved, we hope that we have emphasised the importance of oral testimony to development and shown that much can be gained from it by listener and narrator alike. Above all, oral testimony work serves to amplify the voices of those living on the "underside of development [2]", ensuring that they are heard and become increasingly influential in the shaping of development.

END PIECE

So shall my word be that goes forth from my mouth;
It shall not return to me empty,
But it shall accomplish that which I purpose,
And prosper in the thing for which I sent it.
Isaiah, 55, v11

One of the problems with the written word is that it tends towards an illusion of completeness—especially when it is sealed up in all the seriousness of a printed book. Because of this, the last chapter can give the mistaken impression of being the last word on a subject. But books are bound and published when the ideas in them are still developing and the experiences they describe are changing daily with new discoveries and fresh interpretations. It would therefore be quite wrong to think that because this book finishes here, we have dealt with all the issues involved in collecting and applying people's oral testimony in the development process. On the contrary, our purpose has been to serve as an introduction to the many different ways in which people are attempting to speak and listen to each other in development work today.

We hope, therefore, that *Listening for a Change* will be treated as an open book. Like the more organic forms of oral artistry, we hope people will change, correct, develop and add to the techniques and experiences outlined in these chapters—and we would be interested to hear about such developments. In the meantime, we have attempted to provide a good cross-section of the experience to date and raise some of the main practical, conceptual and ethical issues which confront people engaged in oral testimony work. The result, however, is in no way intended to be a complete guide. There will be some types of

FURTHER READING

For background reading on the practice of oral testimony collection, we especially recommend the following (for full bibliographical details, see References):

Gluck, S and Patai, D (eds), *Women's Words: the Feminist Practice of Oral History*: includes especially frank discussions on the ethical and practical problems of socially committed research on women.

Thompson, P, *The Voice of the Past: Oral History*: an overview of the philosophy and practice of life story and oral history work, including an extensive bibliography.

Vansina, J, *Oral Traditions as History*: the classic call for the serious use of African oral tradition in history.

In addition:

Bornat, J (ed), *Reminiscence Reviewed: Perspectives, Evaluations, Achievements*, Open University Press, Milton Keynes, UK, 1993: the best recent review of reminiscence work among older people in the health and social services context in Britain.

Henige, D, *Oral Historiography*, Longman, UK, 1982: a useful practical introduction for fieldwork in the South.

Lummis, T, *Listening to History: The Authenticity of Oral Evidence*, Hutchison, London, 1978: on analysing oral evidence, including quantification.

Plummer, K, *Documents of Life: An Introduction to the Problems and Literature of a Humanistic Method*, Unwin Hyman, London, 1983: an introduction for social scientists.

Samuel, R and Thompson, P (eds), *The Myths We Live By*, Routledge & Kegan Paul, London, 1990: an international collection of vivid essays on how people continually reshape community and family memories to make sense of their past and inspire their futures.

CONTACT POINTS

It would be impossible to give all the addresses of the many development and community organisations we contacted in the course of researching this book. The References contain details of certain publications and institutions mentioned in the text, and the following are some additional key contact points and sources of information. For details on other organisations mentioned in the book, please contact Olivia Bennett at Panos.

BRITAIN

British Library National Sound Archive and National Life Story Collection, 29 Exhibition Road, London SW7 2AS. Tel: 071-412 7405. Fax: 071-412 7416. Curator in Oral History: Rob Perks

HelpAge International, St James Walk, London EC1R OBE. Tel: 071-253 0253 Fax: 071-253 4814

International Institute of Environment and Development (IIED), 3 Endsleigh Street, London WC1H. Tel: 071-388 2117 Fax: 071-388 2826

Institute of Development Studies, University of Sussex, Falmer, Brighton BN1 9RE. Tel: O273 606261. Fax: 0273 621202/691647. Robert Chambers

Oral History Society, Department of Sociology, University of Essex, Colchester CO4 3SQ. Tel: 0206 873055. Fax: 0206 873410. Brenda Corti

Save the Children Fund (UK), Mary Datchelor House, 17 Grove Lane, London SE5 8RD. Tel: 071-703 5400. Fax: 071-703 2278. Hugo Slim

SOS Sahel (UK), 1 Tolpuddle Street, London N1 OXT. Tel: 071-837 9129. Fax: 071-837 0856. Nigel Cross

BRAZIL

Museu da Pessoa, Rua Cardeal Arcoverde, São Paulo. Tel: 814 4912. Karen Worcman

CPDOC, Fundação Gelulio Vargas, Rio de Janeiro 9052 ZC02. Tel: 551 0847. Angela de Castro Gomez

CHINA

Department of History, University of Peking, Beijing. Professor Yang Li-Wen

HUNGARY

Sociological Institute, 1080 Budapest V. Tel: 155 2190. András Kovács

MEXICO

Instituto de Investigaciones Dr Jose Maria Luis Mora, Plaza Valentin Gomez Farias 12, San Juan 03730, Mexico DF. Tel: 598 3777. Graciela de Garay

SINGAPORE

Oral History Department, University of Singapore, 140 Hill Street, Singapore 0617. Daniel Chew

SOUTH AFRICA

Department of History, University of Cape Town, Rondesbosch. Colin Bundy

UNESCO

CLT/DEC-UNESCO, 7 Place de Fontenoy, 75700 Paris, France. Tel: 331-4568 1000. Mr F Childe

UNITED STATES

Oral History Association, 1093 Broxton Avenue, No 720, Los Angeles, California 90024. Tel: 310-825 0597. Fax: 310-206 1864. Richard Candida Smith

REFERENCES

CHAPTER 1

1. Watson, H, *Women in the City of the Dead*, C Hurst and Co., London, 1992, p11.
2. Tannen, D, *You Just Don't Understand: Women and Men in Conversation*, Virago, London, Chapter 3, 1992.
3. Spender, D, *Man-made Language*, Routledge & Kegan Paul, London, 1980.
4. Watson, H, op. cit.
5. Cross, N and Barker, R (eds), *At The Desert's Edge: Oral histories from the Sahel*, Panos Books, London, 1991, p16.

CHAPTER 2

1. Staunton, I (ed), *Mothers of the Revolution*, Baobab Books, Harare, Zimbabwe, 1990.
2. In all these various forms, oral history has grown rapidly in the North over the last 20 years. It now has its own societies and journals in several countries, such as *Oral History* in Britain, *Bios* in Germany, *Oral History Review* in the USA and *Historia y Fuente Oral* in Spain, and a new *International Yearbook of Oral History and Life Stories* as well as regular international conferences. These developments have certainly not been confined to the North. There are regional international oral history journals funded by UNESCO in the Spanish Caribbean and in Southern Africa, as well as academics practising oral history in many Latin American and African countries, and some in the Far East. A number of African countries have state-funded oral archives, as do Indonesia, Malaysia and, most generously of all, Singapore—a model programme for both North and South.
3. Vargas Llosa, M, *The Storyteller*, Faber and Faber, London, 1991.
4. See Vansina, J, *Oral Tradition as History*, James Currey, London, and Heinemann Kenya, 1985.
5. Ibid.
6. Feierman, S, *The Shambaa Kingdom*, University of Wisconsin Press, Madison, 1974.
7. Adams, C (ed), *Across Seven Seas and Thirteen Rivers: Life stories of pioneer Sylheti settlers in Britain*, THAP books, London, 1987.
8. Lewis, O, *The Children of Sanchez*, Random House, New York, 1961.
9. Lewis, O, *Pedro Martinez*, Random House, New York, 1964.

CHAPTER 3

1. Chambers, R, *Rural Development: Putting the Last First*, Longman, London, 1983; and *Challenging the Professions: Frontiers for rural development*, Intermediate Technology Publications, London, 1993; see also Cernea, M, *Putting People First: Sociological Variables in Rural Development*, Oxford University Press, 1991.
2. Rhoades, R, "The role of farmers in the creation of agricultural technology", in Chambers, R, Pacey, A and Thrupp, L, *Farmer First: Farmer innovation and agricultural research*, Intermediate Technology Publications, London, 1989.

3. Wilson, K, "Indigenous conservation in Zimbabwe: soil erosion, land-use planning and rural life", paper presented to the African Studies Association's conference on Conservation and Rural People, Cambridge, September 1988.
4. Robinson, P, "Reconstructing Gabbra history and chronology: time reckoning, the Gabbra calendar and the cyclical view of life", in Downing, T (ed), *Coping with Drought in Kenya*, L Rienner, USA, 1989.
5. Vaughan, M, *The Story of an African Famine: Gender and Famine in Twentieth Century Malawi*, Cambridge University Press, 1987.
6. De Waal, A, *Famine that Kills: Darfur, Sudan 1984-85*, Oxford University Press, 1989.
7. Nunes, J, "Peasants and survival: the social consequences of displacement, Mocuba, Zambezia", unpublished, Refugee Studies Programme, Oxford, 1992.
8. Ryle, J, "The meaning of survival for the Dinka of Sudan", paper presented to the National Life Story Collection's Oral History and Development Conference, London, November 1991.
9. Slim, H, "A Report on the Harare Workshop on Family Tracing", Save the Children Fund, Harare, May 1992.
10. Quoted in Wadden, M, *Nitassinan: The Innu struggle to reclaim their homeland*, Douglas & McIntyre, Vancouver, Canada, 1991, p78.
11. *Gathering Voices: Finding strength to help our children*, Innu Nation and the Mushuau Innu Band Council, Utshimasits, Ntesinan, June 1992, p1.
12. Ibid., pp4 and 6.
13. Mupedziswa, R, "Elderly camp refugees and social development: traditional status—a salient dimension compromised?", paper presented to the HelpAge workshop on "Change and Development Through Workshops", Harare, Zimbabwe, 1989.
14. Scott, I, "Only Stories and Songs? The People's Educational Association of Sierra Leone", unpublished MA dissertation, Reading University, 1992.
15. Namibia Development Briefing, Vol 2, No 3, 1992.
16. Hayes, P, *Speak for Yourself*, Longman Namibia, 1992, p13.
17. See *Panoscope*, No 27, Panos, London, November 1991.
18. Mavro, A, "Development theatre: a way to listen. A report on the community environment project's development theatre, Tominian, Mali", SOS Sahel, London, 1992.
19. Kanaana, S, "The role of women in *intifadah* legends", paper presented to the Discourse on Palestine conference, University of Amsterdam, April 1992.
20. Panos is currently working with development and other organisations in some eight countries, collecting interviews to explore the wider impacts of conflict on women, as part of its Oral Testimony Information Programme.
21. Africa Watch's 1990 report, *Somalia, A Government at War With its Own People: testimonies about the killings and the conflict in the north*, is an example of the approach which mixes extensive oral

testimony and individual histories with a wider legal and political analysis. See also Ardill, N and Cross, N, *Undocumented Lives*, Runnymede Trust, 1988, for which immigrant workers in the UK were interviewed, as part of a campaign to influence the Immigration Bill.

22. Coleridge, P, *Disability, Liberation and Development*, Oxfam in association with Action on Disability and Development, Oxford, 1993.

23. Warner, R, *Voices from Somalia*, Minority Rights Group, London, 1991.

24. Chambers, R, "Shaping the Past: people's maps, models and diagrams in local historical analysis and planning", a paper presented to the National Life Story Collection's conference on oral history and development, London, November 1991. See also Chambers, R, "Rural Appraisal: Rapid, Relaxed and Participatory", IDS Discussion Paper 311, Institute of Development Studies, Sussex, England, 1992.

25. For a more detailed discussion, see *Forced to Move: large development projects and forced resttlement*, Panos Media Briefing No 5, Panos, London, 1993.

26. Gulati, L, *Fisherwomen on the Kerala Coast*, Women, Work and Development Series, International Labour Office, Geneva, 1984.

27. *Honey Bee*, Vol 3, Nos 3 and 4, Indian Institute of Management, Ahmedabad, India, Aug-Dec 1992, p15. The Society for Research and Initiatives for Sustainable Technologies and Institutions (SRISTI) is at the same address and aims to steer global efforts towards documenting and valuing indigenous innovations.

28. Richards, P, *Indigenous Agricultural Revolution*, Hutchison & Co, London, 1985, cited in *A Plague of Locusts—Special Report*, US Congress, Office of Technology Assessment, OTA-F-450, Government Printing Office, Washington DC, July 1989, p103.

29. Wilson, K, op. cit.

30. Nunes, J, op. cit.

31. Project document, HelpAge International, London, UK.

32. Mavro, A, op. cit.

33. Gubbels, P and Kwéné, N, "Rural theatre for integrated development", evaluation report, SOS Sahel, London, May 1993.

34. Conquergood, D, "Health theatre in a Hmong refugee camp: performance, communication and culture", *TDR: Journal of Performance Studies*, 32, No 3 (T119), Fall 1988, pp174-208.

35. Burt, B, "Land rights and development: writing about Kwara'ae tradition", *CS Quarterly*, 15 (2), pp61-64.

36. Ibid.

37. Ibid.

38. Brody, H, *Maps and Dreams: Indians and the British Columbia Frontier*, Faber and Faber, London, 1981 (revised edition, Penguin, 1986), pxv.

39. Ibid. The full findings can be consulted in volumes 16-17 of the transcripts of the Northern Pipeline Agency's 1979 hearings.

40. Ibid., pp146-7.
41. Ibid., p148.
42. Ibid., p175.
43. Ibid., pp176-7.
44. Ibid., p148.

CHAPTER 4
1. Briggs, C, *Learning How To Ask: A Sociolinguistic Appraisal of the Role of the Interview in Social Science Research*, Cambridge University Press, 1986.
2. Mitchell, J and Slim, H, "Listening to rural people in Africa: the semi-structured interview in rapid rural appraisal", *Disasters*, Vol 15, No 1, March 1991.
3. Norberg-Hodge, H, *Ancient Futures: Learning From Ladakh*, Rider Books, London, 1991, p36.
4. Lomo Zachary in a letter to Ken Wilson, Refugee Studies Programme, Oxford, 1987.
5. Briggs, C, op. cit.
6. Mitchell, J and Slim, H, "Interviewing amidst fear", unpublished paper, Rural Evaluations, 1990.
7. See also the introduction to Cross, N and Barker, R (eds), *At The Desert's Edge: Oral histories from the Sahel*, Panos Books, London, 1991.
8. See Bornat, J, "The communities of community publishing", *Oral History*, Vol 20, No 2, Autumn 1992.
9. Kumar, K, "Conducting group interviews in developing countries", A.I.D. Program Design and Evaluation Methodology Report No 8, US Agency for International Development, Washington, 1987.
10. N'Diaye, P, *Oral Tradition, in Cultural Development: Some Regional Experiences*, UNESCO, Paris, 1981, quoted in Scott, I, "Only Stories and Songs? The People's Educational Association of Sierra Leone", unpublished MA dissertation, Reading University, 1992.
11. Finnegan, R, "A note on oral tradition and historical evidence", in Dunaway, D and Baum, W, *Oral History: An Interdisciplinary Anthology*, American Association for the Study of Local History, Nashville, 1984.
12. Vaughan, M, *The Story of an African Famine: Gender and Famine in Twentieth Century Malawi*, Cambridge University Press, 1987, p121.
13. Articles 12 and 13 of the United Nations Convention on the Rights of the Child, United Nations, 1989.
14. See Garbarino, J and Stott, F, *What Children Can Tell Us*, Jossey-Bass Inc., US, 1989.
15. Richman, N, *Communicating with Children: Helping Children in Distress*, Save the Children Fund (UK), London, 1993.
16. See Garbarino, J and Stott, F, op. cit.
17. Richman, N, op. cit, pp55-57.
18. Webb, B, *My Apprenticeship*, Longman, London, 1926, pp361-2.
19. Mitchell, J and Slim, H, "Hearing Aids for Interviewing", *RRA*

Notes, No 9, International Institute for Environment and Development (IIED), London, August 1990.

20. The details about the Native American talking-stick are taken from a talk given by the American storyteller, Richard Cupidi, at Intermediate Technology's 1992 Annual Public Meeting, London.

21. See Chambers, R, "Shaping the Past: people's maps, models and diagrams in local historical analysis and planning", a paper presented to the National Life Story Collection's conference on Oral History and Development, London, November 1991.

22. See, for example, Chambers, R, "Rural Appraisal: Rapid, Relaxed and Participatory", IDS Discussion Paper 311, Institute of Development Studies, Sussex, England, 1992.

23. Devararam, J et al, "PRA for rural resource management", *RRA Notes*, No 13, 1991, cited in Chambers, R, "Shaping the Past", op. cit. IIED training materials and *RRA Notes* are useful sources of information on PRA and RRA methods in practice.

24. "Farmer participatory research in north Omo, Ethiopia", a report on a training course in Rapid Rural Appraisal, Soddo, July 1991, IIED and FARM Africa, London, cited in Chambers, R, "Shaping the Past", op. cit.

25. Chambers, R, "Shaping the Past", op. cit.

26. Pretty, J N, McCracken, J A, McCauley, D S, and Mackie, C, *Agroecosystem Training and Analysis in Central and East Java, Indonesia*, IIED, London, 1988, cited in Chambers, R, "Shaping the Past", op. cit.

27. Venu Prasad, A, in Chambers, R, "Shaping the Past", op. cit.

28. Chambers, R, "Shaping the Past", op. cit.

29. See Theis, J and Grady H, "PRA for community development", IIED and SCF (UK), 1991; and Leurs, R, "A resource manual for trainers and practitioners of PRA", Overseas Aid Group, Birmingham University, UK, 1993.

30. Kasente, D H, "The impact of the Uganda Women's Tree-Planting Movement at the grassroots", Department of Women's Studies, Makerere University, Uganda, June 1992.

31. Quoted in Nathaniel, L and Sanater, H N, "First steps to recovery: Urban surveys in Somaliland, Part II", Save the Children Fund (UK), 1993.

CHAPTER 5

Case Study 1

1. LaFond, A, "The history of immunisation in Somalia from a community perspective", paper presented to the National Life Story Collection's Conference on Oral History and Development, London, November 1991.

2. LaFond, A, "A study of immunisation acceptability in Somalia", Save the Children Fund (UK), April 1990. This report and the paper cited above are the source for all the information and quotes in this case study.

Case Study 2
1. *Folha de São Paulo*, 10 November, 1991.
2. Belmiro de Santana.
3. Lurdes Grzybowski.
4. *Pina Povo Cultura Memoria*, Centro de Cultura Luiz Freire, 1990.
5. I owe a special debt to Ana Dourado, not only for first drawing my interest to the Recife community projects during her year at the University of Essex, but also for her generous practical help, encouragement and hospitiality during my two visits to Recife. I also wish to thank Antonio Montenegro, Têda Ventura and Moisès de Melho for all the information and help which they gave me on Casa Amarela. Lastly, I am grateful to both the British Council and HelpAge International for their contributions to my travel costs.

Case Study 3
1. This case-study was drawn from material in Johnson, M (ed), *Lore: Capturing Traditional Environmental Knowledge*, Dene Cultural Institute and International Development Research Centre, Ottawa, Canada, 1992, pp35-68; Johnson, M, "Documenting Dene Traditional Environmental Knowledge", *Akwe:kwon Journal*, Vol IX, No 2, Summer 1992, Cornell University, New York, pp72-79; and Johnson, M and Ruttan, R, "Traditional Dene Environmental Knowledge: a pilot project conducted in Fort Good Hope and Colville Lake, NWT, 1989-1993", Dene Cultural Institute, Hay River, NWT, Canada.
2. Bella T'seleie, 1990.
3. Hycinth Kochon, 1990.
4. Richard Kochon, 1985.
5. Zieba, R, "Healing and Healers among the Northern Cree", Masters thesis, Natural Resources Institute, University of Manitoba, Winnipeg, Canada, 1990.

Case Study 4
1. See Cross, N and Barker, R (eds), *At The Desert's Edge: Oral histories from the Sahel*, Panos Books, London, 1991, px.
2. The quotes in this case study are taken from the interviews gathered in the SOHP, an edited selection of which are contained in Cross, N and Barker, R (eds), *At The Desert's Edge*, op. cit.
3. For a more detailed discussion of this point, see the introduction, Cross, N and Barker, R (eds), *At The Desert's Edge*, op. cit.
4. *Grasshoppers and Locusts: The plague of the Sahel*, Panos Books, London, 1993. Other publications which made direct use of the interviews include Cross, N, *The Sahel: The people's right to development*, Minority Rights Group, London, 1990; and *Greenwar: environment and conflict in the Sahel*, Panos Books, London, 1991.
5. Cross, N and Barker, R (eds), *At The Desert's Edge*, op. cit.
6. The PEP has prepared a glossary and annotated bibliography on participatory methods, with special reference to monitoring and evaluation (available from SOS Sahel).

CHAPTER 6

1. For a more detailed discussion of the nature of memory, see Thompson, P, *The Voice of the Past: Oral History*, Oxford University Press, second edition, 1988, pp110-117.

2. Feierman, S, *The Shambaa Kingdom*, University of Wisconsin Press, Madison, 1974, p15.

3. Pait V, S, *Propiedad, Participación y Solidaridad*, Ediciones INPET, Santa Cruz, Peru, 1992.

4. Vaughan, M, *The Story of an African Famine: Gender and Famine in Twentieth Century Malawi*, Cambridge University Press, 1987, p1.

5. See Mitchell, J and Slim, H, "The Bias of Interviewing", *RRA Notes*, No 10, IIED, London, February 1991.

6. Cross, N and Barker, R (eds), *At The Desert's Edge: Oral histories from the Sahel*, Panos Books, London, 1991, p9.

7. See Tannen, D, *You Just Don't Understand: Women and Men in Conversation*, Virago Press, London, 1992. See also Gluck, S and Patai, D (eds), *Women's Words: The Feminist Practice of Oral History*, Routledge & Kegan Paul, London, 1991.

8. Thompson, P, *The Voice of the Past*, op. cit.

9. Abrams, R, *Woman In A Man's World: Pioneering Career Women of the Twentieth Century*, Methuen, London, 1993, pxvii.

10. Vargas Llosa, M, *The Storyteller*, Faber and Faber, London, 1991, p32.

11. The interviewing was undertaken as part of a Panos oral testimony project into "Women and Conflict", to be completed and published in 1994.

12. Daphne Patai has written particularly graphically about her unease in this sense when working with women in Brazilian *favelas*. See Gluck, S and Patai, D (eds), *Women's Words*, op. cit.

13. Portelli, S, *History Workshop Journal*, No 12, 1981, p100, quoted in Thompson, P, *The Voice of the Past*, op. cit. p139.

14. Pait V, S, op. cit.

15. Reynolds, P and Crawford Cousins, C, *Lwaano Lwanyika: Tonga Book of the Earth*, Panos Books, London, 1993.

END PIECE

1. Mohammed, A,"What can focus groups really tell us?", paper presented at the Save the Children Workshop on Information Work in East Africa, Addis Ababa, September 1993.

2. A phrase adapted from the writings of the liberation theologian, Gustavo Gutierrez, who refers to those living on " the underside of history".

INDEX

between environment and development in such areas, as well as the changing social and economic conditions. The third phase aims to uncover the experiences and difficulties faced by people who have been resettled as a result of large development projects, and so to explore the implications of past failures and successes in *resettlement* programmes. In each project, the many different communities and organisations we work with generate the topics to be explored, gain the skills and experience to undertake an oral testimony project, and can use and build on the resulting material in whatever ways they see fit.

Panos will publish a book on each issue, based on the testimonies, backed up with analysis, comment and background information. We will at the same time be monitoring and evaluating the methods and issues involved in oral testimony collection, interpretation, presentation and use in a development context. We would very much like to hear from any groups, particularly in the South, who are already working in this area or are interested in so doing, and who would like to share their experiences and/or learn from other groups and individuals.

We hope that the series—authored by non-authors who are professionals in their own lives and societies—will inform and even reform development debate, policy and practice.

Olivia Bennett (Panos)
Programme director

Nigel Cross (SOS Sahel)
Programme consultant
October 1993

The Panos Oral Testimony Programme

There are many ways to benefit from the knowledge that belongs to the poor, to minorities, to the powerless: the anthropology student gains a PhD and academic advancement; the development consultant signs another tax-free contract; the photo-journalist copyrights the exotic human image; the environmentalist wins a prime-time sound-bite. But what of those who freely share their views and experience?

The aim of the Panos Oral Testimony Programme is to publish and amplify the voices and opinions of the "subjects" of development—people who want to speak for themselves, and not be heard through the distorting medium of outside "experts". Oral testimonies are vivid, personal and direct; they challenge the generalisations and platitudes of so much development rhetoric; they enlighten planners and politicians about what it feels like to be at the sharp end of development.

The programme was launched with the publication of SOS Sahel's collection of oral testimonies on environmental change in the Sahel. *At The Desert's Edge*, published in English, French and Dutch, "demonstrates the value and utility of collecting oral history and applying the resulting material in a manner useful to the people who provided it....It should be required reading for any researcher preparing for...interviewing African informants." (*Journal of African History*.) The second title in the series is *Listening for a Change*, which is both an account of the uses of oral testimony in a development context, and a practical guide designed to encourage and promote oral testimony collection.

The Panos programme also aims to increase understanding of certain specific development issues through the collection and dissemination of oral testimony. Working with local development and community organisations in many different countries, Panos is already gathering interviews on *women and conflict*. The aim is to enable women to articulate their own experiences, perceptions and concerns about the many different impacts of conflict and their views on recovery and rehabilitation.

In 1993, work started on collecting oral testimonies from a variety of communities living in *highland regions*—from the *altiplano* of Bolivia to the Himalayan foothills—and communicating their views on the fragile relationship